INSIDE THE BOARDROOM

Praise for the book

'Many boards as well as advisers to boards labour under the misapprehension that a value-adding board is one whose members are only conversant with laws, rules and regulations that govern the functioning of the corporate entity. Behavioural aspects often do not feature in such conversations. Gopal and his co-author have focused on this important aspect of the functioning of boards and the contribution of directors in this latest offering to the corporate world. The book, in the no-holds-barred style of the authors, has rightly placed behavioural aspects centre stage and established that absent this aspect, boards will continue to perform suboptimally.'

—**M. Damodaran**, former chairman, SEBI, UTI and IDBI

'This book is a must-read to understand how boards work and the behavioural practices of real-life corporate governance. It emphasizes four key points. First, study the company whose board you serve on and the sector in which it operates. Second, see everything that happens in the board and committee meetings without missing a trick. Third, smell things around you because, like stale fish, companies and boards going downhill smell. Fourth, speak without fear or favour when necessary. An independent director must always remember that the adjective 'independent' is valuable. Board members and practitioners will find this book worth their while.'

—**Dr Omkar Goswami**, chairman, CERG Advisory Private Limited

'Mr Gopalakrishnan brings the sheer weight of his decades of experience of running companies and serving on boards of iconic companies to share several insights on governance. The book will be valuable for anyone looking to improve their understanding of corporate governance in the modern business world.'

—**N. Chandrasekaran**, chairman, Tata Sons

'R. Gopalakrishnan, with his rich boardroom experience spanning over three decades, and Tulsi Jayakumar, with her keen understanding of economics, business academia and behavioural issues, bring alive the skills and behaviours that make good governance and caution against the pitfalls on the road to governance. In their inimitable and easy style, they not only reflect on some of the infamous examples of corporate mis-governance but also offer sound practical solutions. With exciting anecdotes and insightful learnings, this is a book every leader across the spectrum of business corporations to public life—current or aspiring—should read.'

—**Sanjiv Mehta**, CEO and managing director,
Hindustan Unilever Limited

INSIDE THE BOARDROOM

How Behaviour Trumps Rationality

R. GOPALAKRISHNAN
TULSI JAYAKUMAR

RUPA

Published by
Rupa Publications India Pvt. Ltd 2023
7/16, Ansari Road, Daryaganj
New Delhi 110002

Sales centres:
Bengaluru Chennai Hyderabad
Jaipur Kathmandu Kolkata
Mumbai Prayagraj

P-ISBN: 978-93-5702-512-6
E-ISBN: 978-93-5702-514-0

First impression 2023

10 9 8 7 6 5 4 3 2 1

Contents

Preface

Corporate governance is not only about boardroom processes but also about behaviours that promote transparent decision-making on corporate issues considering the perspective of all stakeholders. Although the expression 'corporate governance' was not invented during ancient times, the concept is exemplified by the four-point Vedantic exhortation about 'doing well by doing good'. These exhortations are improving self-awareness, protecting all resources that enable business, serving others and being compassionate to stakeholders.

Note that the emphasis in this definition is on processes and behaviours—both influence outcomes. Too much process-orientation without a sound understanding of behaviour, or the other way around, produces unexpected outcomes. That is what this book is about—process plus behaviour.

Governance Guides

In practice, corporate governance seems to be much more about processes and rules, with scant acknowledgement of the influence of human behaviour on it. In the discourse about corporate governance, there is an almost exclusive emphasis on rules, processes and laws. Yet, as all directors know, the elephant in the room is behaviour. It is rooted in culture, customs, habits and perspectives—elements of our subconscious—but they vary for each director and are prone to being stereotypical. How does one optimally blend behaviours with regulations and processes to yield a professional corporate culture that leads to strong and positive governance?

Both in India and abroad, several corporate governance failures have occurred despite corporate laws and regulations being strengthened. Stories of bitter fights between brothers, relatives or even long-term partners have emerged from behind the closed doors of the boardroom and made national headlines. Scions of prominent business families develop irreconcilable differences of opinion and separate for peace and profits. Diverging perspectives can and do exist, and if resolved quietly and civilly, they do not attract public debate. However, with alleged mismanagement, infighting and financial scandal, adverse publicity, heartbreak and acrimony follow.

Since antiquity, families have fought behind closed doors, on the battlefield or even in the courts of law in contemporary times. If families, as the smallest unit of society, are prone to being misgoverned, what does it mean for the corporate sector in a time when regulatory frameworks for accountability and compliance are being strengthened globally? Are governance failures inevitable, despite increasing regulations and laws? Perhaps not.

It is true that regulation and public commentary have become increasingly effective, and that is the good news. Yet, stronger rules for better governance under the watchful media eye have not decreased transgressions. Is there a missing link that goes beyond the arcane language of and brouhaha around corporate governance? The answer may well lie in human behaviour rather than rational laws. There is a significant difference between *neeti*, *neeyat* and *niyam*—conduct, intent and rules.

A mythological story has been presented below as an allegory to connect corporate governance with the behavioural aspects of what happens within the boardroom. After all, isn't behaviour rooted in social and cultural soils?

An Epic Metaphor

The themes and story of the Mahabharata, one of India's greatest epics, are well-known. Many may view the Mahabharata as being rather lengthy (it is several times longer than both the Greek epics—Iliad and Odyssey—put together), representing the propensity of Indians to impart a key message in an indirect or roundabout manner. However, we can take away key lessons from the epic if it is creatively interpreted as an allegory, with the characters being seen as board members of a mythical corporation. Their behaviours may be applied to the boardroom, in-line with the way their personalities have been depicted in the original story.

Imagine, the hundred Kauravas and five Pandavas serve as directors of the family business called KP Corporation. This corporation serves the *praja* (people) or the shareholders. Their purpose is wealth generation and protection of the praja through good governance. The executive directors and non-executive directors on the KP board help achieve this goal. An underlying distrust compels both factions of the Kauravas and Pandavas to keep a watchful eye on one another.

The non-executive chairman (NEC) of this corporation is Dhritarashtra, the patriarch of the Kaurava clan, who is blind and relies on Sanjaya, the company secretary, to keep him informed about company affairs. Sanjaya has the insight to see everything but hesitates to make a complete report, especially when something seems to be amiss.

Dhritarashtra's son, Duryodhana desperately wishes to be heir to the KP empire. Dhritarashtra, of course, has named Yudhishthira—his deceased elder brother, Pandu's eldest son—as the crown prince. Dhritarashtra is mostly well-intentioned but somewhat ineffective.

He is overwhelmed by his strong-willed son and managing director (MD) Duryodhana, who dominates the board and the mind of the chairman. Duryodhana is self-obsessed, with an aggressive and competitive spirit. He works with three executive directors from the Pandava clan, whose loyalty he constantly doubts.

The finance director is Duryodhana's Pandava cousin, Yudhishthira—the designated crown prince who is morally upright, thoughtful and observant amid the transactional turmoil. Yudhishthira is also perceived as the person who understands what is best for the organization and knows what needs to be done. The aggressive marketing director is another Pandava, Arjuna, a fine professional much prized and valued for a sharp instinct and skill. Arjuna is proud and fully aware of the admiration the team has for him. The supply chain director is also a Pandava, Bhima, a picture of strength, reliability and precise operational delivery. He is pushy, efficient and achieves his targets.

There are two non-executive family directors, of whom Shakuni, the MD's maternal uncle, is prominent. He is crafty and devious and constantly plotting to enable Duryodhana to become the successor to the KP empire. He has the MD's ear and whispers dubious stories to Duryodhana. The other non-executive director from the family is Karna, who is a good manager and Duryodhana's best friend. Being grateful to Duryodhana for past favours, he is the MD's yes-man. As Duryodhana's loyal subordinate, Karna typifies a myrmidon with his total commitment and willingness to carry out orders unquestioningly.

The general counsel of the board is Krishna, a strategic kingmaker who favours the Pandavas. He is worldly and knowledgeable. He guides the board and has an astute ability to convince others based on a deep perspicacity of how to act in the right manner. The trouble is his answers are as confounding as the dilemmas faced by the board, so they cannot deal with his advice without relapsing into deep thought.

Additionally, there are three independent directors to help the board comply with governance regulations. They are regarded as independent due to one principal quality of being emotionally equidistant from both sides of the KP family. Bhishma has rich managerial experience and is wisdom incarnate. He has only one problem: he misses the opportunity to speak up at the right time. Vidura, another independent director, is upright, ethical and hugely valued for his work. There is also a woman director called Kunti, who is an astute and wise professional. However, she is unable to influence the deeper undercurrents in the KP boardroom.

As events in the company unfold, the conflict regarding the high pressure yet unspoken question of succession leads to battle lines being drawn between the Kauravas and the Pandavas. The praja senses mayhem. The developments are meticulously noted by the watchful regulator, Veda Vyasa, who invites the media into the unfolding corporate drama. He dictates notes to his favourite scribe, Ganapati, who diligently records the unfolding saga.

The battle for succession mushrooms into an upheaval that raises many questions among the shareholders relating to the efficacy of the board of directors, the blame game being played out between them and even the motivations of the powerful MD. Why did the independent directors fail to speak up? Why did the regulator not intervene?

This allegory goes to show that a board of directors does not always behave in a manner that promotes the aims of the organization. It points to the fact that interpersonal relations are often more powerful than the purpose of governance.

Behaviour Alters Governance

This mythological allegory has multiple parallels in the real world of corporate transgressions that emphasize the behavioural aspects of corporate governance. History is replete with cases of epic and expensive corporate failures caused not because of any lack of intelligence or skill but because of a social climate inhibiting the free flow of suggestions. If company secretaries or directors do not speak up and deliver unpleasant news, or state a negative possibility whenever a situation demands it, the gap between the decision-makers and the shareholders deepens. This creates an insurmountable silence that can lead to a massive disaster.

We consider directors on a company's board to be rational and logical decision-makers, who speak the truth when necessary. However, as presented in the allegory from the Mahabharata, directors are about as rational as any other human. There is a fair element of subjectivity and behavioural bias in their decision-making. The behavioural and cultural nuances playing out in a boardroom are significant in most incidents of governance failure. Therefore, it is suggested that nomination committees recruiting new board members for their skills should perhaps focus more on hiring directors for their positive attitude, and constructive board behaviour.

It may seem audacious to assert that directors are not entirely rational. However, the distinctive idea underlying this book and its primary message is simply this: directors' 'human' behaviour in the boardroom may majorly contribute to failures in corporate governance. It is an uncommon perspective but directors' human behaviour may lead a company to a moment of truth, when everything spirals into chaos. It is important to note that the affairs of the world are seldom decided upon the evidence of truth. Too often, petty emotionalism governs.

Behaviour is subjective, with infinite expressions. So, while rights may be conferred or duties allocated by law to regulate human behaviour, it cannot be regulated entirely by legislation.

Behaviour is moored in mythology, local culture, social attitudes to power and the hierarchy of authority. These elements frequently show up in most instances of governance failure. Thus, public pressure, awareness campaigns and social techniques may be more effective methods than legislation to introduce behavioural changes. Such behavioural changes evolve slowly, but last longer.

Behaviours, being self-taught, can be changed. So, while directors' unique subjectivities and behavioural biases impact their decisions, it is possible for them to learn how to act in a certain way. If directors can learn the rules and regulations regarding company governance, it is possible for them to learn to behave rationally in the boardroom. This book aims to be a starting point to consider how to influence ethics and behaviour inside the boardroom.

An Outline

The inspiration for this book came from the title of the Tamil translation of R. Gopalakrishnan's first book. The English title of the book was *The Case of the Bonsai Manager*. In Tamil, it was titled *Nirvaga Illaiyil Nijamana Anubhavangal*, which means 'real experiences from the management world'.

This book is based on the experiences gained and observations made by us while navigating events that have happened in the boardrooms of real businesses. We have also drawn upon learnings from public governance and behavioural sciences to bolster our arguments.

The book is intended for everyone interested in governance, whether pertaining to corporations, trusts or public administration, including executives, administrators, directors, aspiring directors and regulators. Our insights are not only applicable in the boardrooms of corporations but also in a wider context. After all, human foibles and behaviours are universal, whether in boardrooms, administrative meetings or political organizations.

This book promises to be an insightful commentary on practical issues, dilemmas and conundrums that impact the corporate world. It interweaves academic findings and practical experiences, and coalesces them into wisdom for board directors. Reflections on real events and experiences are essential for learning. No matter how many rules and regulations a director may master, increasingly, he must also understand the intricacies of behavioural corporate governance. This is what we hope to achieve through the book.

1

Contrary Behaviours

The number of times boards discuss a proposal depends on its nature and financial implications. It is common for new angles to be revealed through such discussions, a bit like unpeeling an onion. This is normal and healthy.

Once, Gopal (R. Gopalakrishnan) served on a company board that repeatedly discussed a proposal to invest in an African country over a span of one year. There was positive business logic to the investment project, but there were severe risks involved with the country. The analytics were presented persuasively by the confident chief executive officer (CEO), who was piloting the proposal. Although the directors did not agitatedly oppose the proposal, they did not acquiesce to it with table-thumping either. However, there were multiple statements of caution, particularly about the country being a risk.

The CEO interpreted the directors' comments as a suggestion to transition to the next stage of exploration. In hindsight, the board's response can be characterized as a weak 'no' rather than a clear 'yes'. Finally, as is often the case with major strategic discussions, it came down to judgement and intuition. After 12 months of deliberation and investigation, the directors agreed not to pursue the investment opportunity based on their collective judgement of the risk.

A few months later, a respected international paper carried an editorial regarding the dire state of that African country. Gopal shared the editorial with several directors with a note stating, 'Thank God we did not proceed with the investment.' The individual response received from the other directors was quite intriguing. Most said, 'I said so while opposing the proposal.' If everyone had opposed the proposal clearly, why had the project been discussed over 12 long months?

The answer, as postulated by one director, lay in the highly respected image of the board chairman. The directors' perception of the chairman being supportive of the proposal muted their opposition to it so much that their message was completely lost.

This is an example of how behaviour trumps rationality in boardroom governance—in this case, fortunately, with no negative fallout. It is actually the incidents of corporate failure, bankruptcy and fall from grace that hold the roots of governance as we know it today.

Common Corporate Code

Thirty years ago, 'corporate governance' was only mentioned in the hallowed halls of accounting and finance.

In 1990, in the United Kingdom (UK), Coloroll (a wallpaper company) and Asil Nadir's Polly Peck (a textile company), collapsed financially due to excessive debt. To prevent the recurrence of business failures like these, the London Stock Exchange set up the Cadbury Committee. Just when this committee had been constituted in May 1991, two more financial disasters hit the market: the collapse of the Bank of Credit and Commerce International (BCCI), and the posthumous discovery of media mogul Robert Maxwell's fraudulent appropriation of a large sum from his company's pension fund. The shock waves from these incidents heightened the sense of urgency underlying the Cadbury Committee's work.

The committee's draft report was made public in May 1992. It prescribed various regulations and processes. The ideas in the draft report were attacked from many quarters. Taking the criticism into account, a redesigned code was published in December 1992. The committee's final report, 'The Financial Aspects of Corporate Governance'[1], better known as the Cadbury Report, set out recommendations about the arrangement of company boards and accounting systems to mitigate corporate governance risks and failures. It also issued a code of best practices.

It was a voluntary code and made four primary recommendations:

1. separating of the roles of the CEO and the board chair;
2. the majority of the board being outside directors;
3. non-executive directors being in the majority on the remuneration committee to restrain senior executives' remuneration;
4. a corporation's audit committee having at least three non-executive directors who can actively engage with the company accounts departments and auditors.

This landmark report became the basis for adoption of a suitable code of corporate governance by several international bodies, like the Organisation for Economic Co-operation and Development (OECD), European Union (EU) and the World Bank. Its basic framework is used till date, with tweaks and updates for the time period and the country where the code has been adopted. For instance, in India, the recommendation to have a board that comprises mostly independent directors has not been adopted.

---

[1]Cadbury, A., *Report of the Committee on the Financial Aspects of Corporate Governance*, Gee, London, 1992.

Watching the Watchdog

How does one watch the watchdog? The greed of audit firms compromising their professional conduct has become a source of serious governance concerns over the years.

The United States of America (US) faced business insolvency with such a twist. In 2002, a $180-billion telecommunication company called Worldcom filed for bankruptcy. It was being audited by a firm called Arthur Andersen, which had been the auditor of Enron (another company that had collapsed a few years earlier). The Securities and Exchange Commission (SEC) highlighted the gross inadequacies in the auditing of the firm. It ruled that the auditing firm did not carry out the essential tests required of a professional audit firm.

The consequent train of events led to the adoption of the Sarbanes–Oxley Act of 2002 in the US, which established sweeping auditing and financial regulations for public companies. Unfortunately, even then, the scandals continued: mortgaging giant Freddie Mac had to pay a penalty and was compelled to correct its accounting processes in 2003; the insurance company AIG was charged with selling fake policies in 2005; the Lehman Brothers filed for bankruptcy, brought down by the collapse of the subprime mortgage market in 2008; and Bernie Madoff designed the largest Ponzi scheme in history in 2008.

A similar pattern can be seen in several countries, for governance has always been a work in progress.

The Scandal Effect

After 32 years of corporate governance being implemented in many countries, have things improved? In India, the Securities and Exchange Board of India (SEBI) has constituted several committees to review governance, and to suggest improvements and better alignment with practices to disable transgressions. Although there have been some negative comments on the progress of corporate governance, we believe that it has progressively improved.

During the last 30 years, major corporations across the globe have undertaken multiple transformations to adapt to shifts in the market forces, be it through new technology or even demands for governance. Various factors have contributed to the metamorphosis, particularly the advent of abundant and cheap capital since the 1980s. Capital has gradually been reoriented towards the short-term, with a view towards quick and significant returns. Greed has taken charge and brought ambitious venture capitalists to the table. They have pushed for increasing eyeballs and market shares instead of common-sense business economics, which has become a key feature of the cheap money era.

There have also been substantial improvements in reporting detail, even though there is a constant clamour for more value-addition from institutional investors and independent directors. Truth be told, there is a fundamental asymmetry of information between executive and non-executive directors. No category of external investors is as familiar with the specifics of the business as the operating executives. The board of directors is required to act along the four pillars of governance—fairness, accountability, responsibility and transparency.

Whether the regulatory and national responses for stricter corporate governance have succeeded, is a subject of commentary and debate among management strategists and writers. Although, business misfortunes cannot be pinned exclusively on a failure of corporate governance, there can be no doubt that adjusting to new demands has also played an indeterminate role in the transformation of corporate governance. There are multiple examples of businesses declining due to corporate reorganization:

1. The confectionary company, Cadbury, had Quaker origins in England in 1924. A responsible and conservative company for over 40 years, it became an important force in British industry. In 1969, it merged with a more aggressive, shareholder-wealth-oriented drink manufacturer, Schweppes. Some analysts state that the character of the company morphed after this merger. The company has been continually reorganized since then. Today, a part of the company rests with American multinational corporation (MNC) Mondelez.

2. Imperial Chemical Industries was a chemical manufacturing giant throughout the twentieth century. Its major growth engine, pharmaceuticals, was spun off as Zeneca and continues to prosper as AstraZeneca. The balance of its portfolio—including commodity products, like petrochemicals, specialty chemicals and decorative paints—has been rearranged, including some significant sales. The paints business is now called AkzoNobel.

3. The market capitalization of General Electric (GE)—acclaimed as the highest valued company in the US in the 1990s—has dropped from $600 billion to about one fourth of its market capitalization due, in part, to corporate reorganization.

Governance in India

In India, too, corporate governance has advanced significantly in the last 30 years. Although, it is still a work in process. As standards and rules of governance have evolved, companies have learnt to adapt and experiment. The Indian stock market, for instance, trades in the stocks of an estimated 5,000 companies. Of these, just about 100 companies account for nearly half of the market capitalization. Thus, the Indian stock market and corporate sector are made up of a stark contrast of a few big players and thousands of smaller ones.

Even among the big players listed in the stock exchange, only some qualify as institutions. These are the players with a track record of progressive practices like succession planning, talent development, critical thinking, long-term value creation for all stakeholders, balancing long-term and short-term approaches, uncontroversial reputation and transparent reporting in the public domain. Such 'institutions' are trusted. Not only does India need more corporate institutions, but it also needs bigger players in the stock market. This too will happen, but in an evolutionary manner.

Gopal, who has served on corporate boards for over 35 years, has had the benefit of a ring-side seat to the evolution of regulatory governance practices and emergence of three types of boards.

Ornamental boards: Until the 1980s, when corporate governance began to be formalized following the recommendations of the Cadbury Committee, boards were often ornamental. This meant that listed companies augmented their boards with well-known individuals just to comply with the newly implemented regulations. Most of these directors were competent and seasoned leaders with a solid reputation. However, since they were only invited to the board for their reputation, not much was expected of them. Hence, they merely had 'ornamental' value. Such reputed but ornamental directors frequently served on so many boards that they were continually rushing from one board meeting to another. At the board meetings, too, they had a short attention span. However, neither these board members nor the company that had invited them were unhappy with this situation.

Soloist boards: Gradually, in response to increasing regulations since the 2000s, some boards advanced to become soloist boards. Company promoters started hiring well-known individuals with a proven track record of expertise in accounting, law, finance, public affairs or international relations. Such distinguished directors could give their views when board discussions featured their area of expertise. Beyond that, the soloist director maintained a low profile and delegated proceedings to the board members with executive responsibility. This was a practical technique to fulfil the regulatory obligation without attracting undue interference from independent directors into executive decisions. Despite the regulatory changes, most promoters believed that the company was theirs, and the soloist directors had to be accessed sparingly for their expertise. Several boards may still be deemed to bear soloist characteristics.

Orchestration boards: Around 2005, increasing incidence of governance failures led to the emergence of orchestration boards, which are still a nascent concept. On these boards, individual directors are expected, individually and collectively, to add value to board decisions. They do so through their ability to take company decisions that are related to broader general management and are based on a societal view. These boards operate on the tenet that the power of many is superior to the power of a few.

Aligning Performance with Compliance

Compliance is, no doubt, crucial for the directors' agenda. It is a critical function of the board. However, if much of the board deliberations focus primarily on compliance, one can justifiably question the strategic and long-term function of the board. The board chairman, executive or non-executive, is endowed with the task of orchestrating the board dynamics and getting the best out of each director.

The collective impact of the board must be greater than the individual impact of each director. If the board is not functioning like an orchestra, its conductor needs to do his or her duty better.

As Andy Grove, founder and board chairman of Intel, reportedly stated, 'The board must ensure that the success of the company is longer lasting than any CEO's reign, than any market opportunity, than any product cycle.'[2]

Corporate India's evolution from ornamental to soloist to orchestrating boards has been a fascinating journey. The difference lies in the detailing. Boards and directors have learnt valuable lessons over the past 30 years, like how to prepare meaningful pre-reading material for the directors' advance study. Sometimes the pre-reading papers are inadequate, and, at other times, excessively detailed. Board discussions are also sometimes too detailed or, at other times, indulging in operational navel-gazing. Every director has participated in and experienced a whole range of presentations—from ones that have no information to ones that have all the necessary information.

An allegory from Paulo Coelho's book *The Alchemist*[3] is relevant in the context of evolving corporate governance. In the story, a father wants his 12-year-old son to grow up to be wise. So, he takes the young boy to a wise man that lives in a mansion atop a hill. The wise man notices the young boy, but, being preoccupied, he asks the boy to walk around his mansion and observe the objects there. He also entrusts the boy with two tablespoons of oil. 'Oh, by the way,' the wise man instructs, 'you must carry the two tablespoons of oil carefully without spilling a drop.'

The diligent boy does as he is asked and returns, mighty pleased that the oil in the tablespoons is intact.

'Did you observe the artefacts in the mansion during your tour?' the wise man asks.

'No, Sir,' the boy responds. 'I was completely focussed on avoiding any spillage of oil.'

---

[2]Schlender, Brent, 'Inside Andy Grove's Latest Crusade', *Fortune*, 23 August 2004, https://tinyurl.com/2kwhe3rr. Accessed on 20 June 2023.
[3]Coelho, Paulo, *The Alchemist*, HarperCollins India, 1998.

'Well then, go back and do another tour. When you return, tell me what you saw and what you liked. And remember not to drop any oil,' the wise man commands.

The boy returns and expresses his wonderment at the intricate sculptures, fine paintings and handicrafts adorning the mansion! Without dropping any oil, he is in awe of what he has seen in the mansion. The wise man advises the boy that this is the secret of wisdom—to pay attention to the small details (of not dropping the oil) while also viewing the big picture and enjoying the wider perspective (of observing the beauty of the mansion).

One cannot underestimate the importance of complete compliance. The sin of omission is as grave as the sin of commissioning errors. The story of the boy and the wise man is instructive and inspiring, especially in the light of governance demands having advanced from ornamental to compliance to strategy. After all, a board of directors is tasked with ensuring that the company's management achieves great performance while being compliant.

Yet, leaders mostly behave in-line with their unstated and intuitive assumptions because, like all humans, they instinctively respond based on certain unconscious algorithms that exist in their minds. For example, one widely accepted and well-tested algorithm states that profit equals revenue minus the costs. That is fine. But the fervour of start-ups in India challenges this assumption, or at least raises the question of whether profit is even necessary.

Another unconscious algorithm states that people's performance comes from their potential minus their obstacles. The obstacles may be visible ones—such as procedural, legal and public policy—or less visible ones rooted in behaviours and attitudes.

Most top managements and even boards are beguiled with the potential, rather than reducing the obstacles. For example, the excitement about alternative sources of renewable energy plays out to a far greater degree than the obstacles to phase out conventional energy.

Cognitive Versus Invisible Signals

In the contemporary discourse on corporate governance, there is an emphasis on its visible and cognitive aspects—regulations related to legal, accounting, risk, cash management, etc. Having served on more than 20 boards in various countries, Gopal has found that in addition to these, the invisible behavioural aspects of corporate governance—inadequate listening skills, disagreements, meaningful participation in strategy or succession planning, interpretation of smoke signals, behavioural oddities and trust-building—merit significant attention.

The invisible aspects of behaviour often go unnoticed because the visible and palpable ones demand immediate attention and action. Even visible behaviours of directors' stem from invisible motivations.

For instance, it is human instinct to seek power, prestige and status contextually. Hence, we act in ways that can elevate our status and win us respect, approval, admiration and acceptance. We intensely desire to belong to a group comprising individuals similar to us. Once we become part of a group, we want to be known. Hence, we tend to emulate behaviours of those we admire or aspire to be. This tendency is evident among newly appointed directors on boards. The new director, who aspires to be a member of the board 'club', for instance, has a strong desire to become an active participant in club activities.

These natural and instinctive motivations direct the functioning of board members too, which generates strong internal pressure within the group. The benefit of being accepted is far greater than the benefit of being right or cautious. Hence, behaviour often trumps the rules and laws that define the role and duties of the independent director, the board chairman and the myriad dos and don'ts for them.

The information technology (IT) company Satyam Computers

was awarded a corporate governance honour just before the dramatic events leading to its collapse unfolded. What can be a better example than an extract from Lehman Brothers Annual Report, just before the company collapsed:

> Lehman Brothers continues to be committed to industry best practices with respect to corporate governance. The company's Board of Directors currently consists of ten members. Except for Mr. Fuld [the CEO], all of the company's directors are independent. [...] The Audit Committee includes a financial expert as defined in the SEC's rules. The Board of Directors holds regularly scheduled executive sessions in which non-management directors meet independently of management. [...] The company has an orientation program for new directors. The company's corporate governance guidelines also contemplate continuing director education arranged by the company. [...] We have a global head of risk management and a global risk management division which is independent. [...] Based on our assessment, we believe that the company's internal controls are effective over financial reporting. These controls have also been considered effective by the independent auditors. We also sponsor several share-based employee incentive plans.[4]

Fortunately, there are early signs and symptoms of such corporate failure that manifest through human behaviour. These can help identify an underlying issue and, if discovered in time, can help prevent a business failure that can negatively impact stakeholders as we shall see in the next chapter.

---

[4]Lehman Brothers, *Annual Report 2007*, 2007, https://tinyurl.com/mfv82bce. Accessed on 4 July 2023.

2

Prodrome: Early Signals of
Governance Failures

To explain a corporate governance failure, we have drawn upon the little-known medical term 'prodrome', which refers to early signs or symptoms that often indicate the onset of a disease before its distinctive manifestation. The word 'prodrome' comes from the Greek word *prodromos*, meaning 'running before'. Prodromes are widely prevalent in nature. For instances, clouds gather in the sky, a cool wind blows with increasing ferocity and it starts drizzling before the break of heavy rain or storm. Even with familial genetic aberrations, some adolescents are known to display odd behaviours as prodromes, before turning to undesirable or dangerous acts.

Portents of Peril

The concept of prodromes is not set in stone. It represents a pattern that has evolved over time. Thus, the distinct observable behavioural changes that characterize a specific disease's prodromal features can provide strong evidence for spotting the onset symptoms of a disease. Understanding the progression of the illness, along with the time span between the onset of prodromal symptoms and the manifestation of the disease, may be important for early detection to prevent the psychological and social disruption caused by the disease.

Consider the missed prodromes in the NASA Hubble Space Telescope (HST) project. The HST was launched in April 1990 to clearly view the stars, planets and galaxies from hitherto unseen angles and perspectives. Shortly after the launch, however, NASA's team discovered that the HST had been launched with a flawed mirror that affected the clarity of early images. This seemingly defeated the purpose of this mission. This led to widespread criticism and a detailed investigation into the matter because a hefty $1.7 billion had been spent on the project and it had been widely publicized. The error was traced back to uncalibrated equipment being used by the vendor PerkinElmer while manufacturing the mirror.

Astonishingly, the flaw in the primary mirror had shown up in the tests conducted at the vendor's plant. The review board wondered why the otherwise competent staff had not rigorously pursued these test discrepancies. It learnt that the highly focussed schedule and budget pressures had caused everyone to move forward relentlessly. Besides, NASA's management of its contractors had been hostile. If vendors could rationalize results, they were not reporting errors. This was a behavioural aberration that remained unacknowledged and unchecked. Vendors had simply grown tired of being rushed and pressured. This led to a seemingly trivial issue in a mirror, overshadowing the accomplishments of thousands of dedicated people and was thought to be a waste of taxpayers' money.

The review board judged this as a leadership failure, not a technical one. An analysis of the gradual progress of the disaster, through an enquiry conducted after the crisis, demonstrated that the advance signals and signs had been visible, but clearly missed. Such signs and symptoms are mostly common among different instances of corporate governance failures. Hence, it is possible for regulators, board members and even the media to be alert for the early warning signs of misgovernance, typically manifested through behavioural aberrations before the failure. Behavioural corporate governance—inspired by economists Amos Tversky and Daniel Kahneman—is an idea whose time has arrived. Kahneman and Tversky demonstrated that the human brain relies on mental shortcuts in decision-making that are rooted in biases, which often leads people to irrational actions.

Consider the case of the German car manufacturer Volkswagen that installed illegal software in its diesel vehicles. This made the vehicles emit more harmful pollutants and violated the Clean Air Act. Volkswagen's Dieselgate scandal about fraudulent emission testing became public in 2015. However, in 2009, *Financial Times* reported about the company 'having the worst corporate governance structure among Germany's blue-chip companies'.[5] There had been much water-cooler talk about this issue too. Yet, all the advance signals—the prodromes—had been missed!

More recently, Wirecard, a Munich-based payment processor and financial services provider, was exposed over a series of corrupt business practices and for undertaking fraudulent financial reporting. This led to the company declaring insolvency. In 2019, the European Securities and Market Authority criticized German regulators for ignoring the red flags over Wirecard's financial reporting for years. News reports carried the headline, 'German regulator should have heeded *Financial Times* on the Wirecard fraud'. Implicitly, doubts were also raised about the role of the independent directors.

---

[5]Schäfer, Daniel, 'VW Governance "Worst" of German Blue Chips', *Financial Times*, 2 December 2009, https://tinyurl.com/4f9eh68s. Accessed on 4 July 2023.

Evidently, ignoring the prodromes of peril has cost businesses dearly in the past. This highlights the urgent need for efficient boards to not only watch out for such warning signs but to also prepare contingency plans based on them.

Defence Mechanisms Against Failures

Globally, corporates appear to be in the throes of governance failures—a disease that has the potential to assume epidemic proportions. Governance failures and the consequent crises have taken root in corporations and become a defining feature of contemporary economies. Such governance crises, brewing or in bloom, can destroy shareholder equity and impact all stakeholders—even society itself.

Corporations have typically addressed their governance issues through rational and hard solutions. This often involves merely checking all the boxes to adhere to corporate governance norms devised by boards. For example, ensuring that the board comprises 'independent' directors, including some women, and having a whistle-blower policy, etc. Such companies also have neatly laid out systems of rewards and punishments to induce desired behaviours among the board members. These solutions are based on economic theories that emphasize rational decision-making. They presume that humans are rational beings who respond to a system of rewards and punishments, based on an appropriate cost–benefit analysis. Tough punishments are assumed to act as a sufficiently strong deterrent. They may be effective, but only as a temporary fix because, fundamentally, misgovernance can be traced back to the human psyche of the board of directors influencing decision-making.

Misgovernance Rooted in Behaviour

Standard economic theory considers man to be rational, a 'homo economicus' who displays utility-maximizing behaviours. A 'rational' man may commit offences to increase personal gains. In other words, he may commit an offence if the probability of being caught multiplied by the penalty imposed for committing the offence is lower than the expected benefit of the infraction.[6] However, this theory of a rational man was recently challenged in a case that shocked the world. It stirred up much debate and discussion from the shores of the US to the tiny brokers' offices on Dalal Street, Mumbai.

Consider the insider trading case against Rajat Gupta, the globally celebrated business leader, who rose through the ranks at McKinsey & Company over 34 years before serving as the management consulting firm's CEO from 1994 to 2003. He was a board member of several well-known corporations, including Goldman Sachs, Procter & Gamble (P&G) and AMR (the parent company of American Airlines), besides being an advisor to Bill Gates. Additionally, he was the chairman of the International Chamber of Commerce and served on the boards of The Wharton School, Harvard University and Massachusetts Institute of Technology's (MIT).

The case dates back to the fall of 2008, when Berkshire Hathaway, owned by Warren Buffet, committed to make a $5 billion investment in Goldman Sachs at a time when public confidence in the company was short. This investment could have provided it the much-needed boost. Seconds after the company's

---

[6]To understand this mathematically, imagine that Mr X is considering whether to accept a bribe of ₹100,000. If caught, he will have to pay a penalty of say ₹50,000. There is a 50 per cent chance of him being caught. Thus, the expected cost of taking the bribe is ₹25,000 (50,000 × 0.5). Since the expected benefit is greater than the expected cost, he will take the bribe.

board concluded their discussion on the investment, Gupta called his friend, Raj Rajaratnam, a hedge fund manager, who apparently traded a sizeable portion of Goldman Sachs' stock before this news was made public. The information passed on by Gupta, as alleged by the SEC, allowed Rajaratnam to profit from these trades.

Rajaratnam defended his purchases stating he had heard that 'something good' might be happening at Goldman Sachs. The SEC alleged that this 'insider trading' had generated more than $18 million in profits and loss avoidance. While Gupta was never found to have directly profited from this information, the SEC noted his involvement with Rajaratnam as an investor in the hedge fund, besides 'other potentially lucrative business interests'.[7] Did Gupta need the money? The answer is a clear 'no'. Gupta's corporate position and social status also indicated that he had no need for access, prestige or any favours.

After conviction and subsequent release from prison, Gupta published the book, *Mind Without Fear*. There, he expressed, on the advice of his lawyers, what he had earlier refrained from stating. He mentioned that an act like calling his business partner Rajaratnam within seconds of a board meeting had most likely nailed the circumstantial evidence against him. However, he also suggested that it was 'normal' to make calls within seconds of concluding a board meeting. Reading the book, one could not help wonder whether he might have lost touch with reality.

Had Gupta been a utility-maximizing homo economicus, he would never have traded his money, prestige and access, for the anticipated gains from such insider trading (which is clearly associated with the risk of loss of freedom). The steep fall from

[7]'SEC Files Insider Trading Charges Against Rajat Gupta, Brings New Charges Against Raj Rajaratnam', *U.S. Securities and Exchange Commission*, 26 October 2011, https://tinyurl.com/eneew3tx. Accessed on 4 July 2023.

grace can, perhaps, be explained by his succumbing to hubris—believing that he could either get away with this action or that the rules of corporate America would not apply to him. In this sense, he did behave irrationally, but it was predictably irrational[8], to borrow a term from behavioural economist Dan Ariely's work.

Reading the Signs

Corporate board failures involve people and, hence, are rooted more in psychological and behavioural factors than in purely economic ones. These crises with a human focus do not appear suddenly but evolve gradually and are usually preceded by prodromes. If directors can be alert to prodromal cues, they can avert the crises.

One way to explore the prodrome is through enquiry. Directors may ask the following questions: Is there good governance? Has the entrepreneur resourced the enterprise with competent management and effective board processes like risk review, audit committee and so on? Is there constructive dissent in board meetings? Does the entrepreneur or promoter display huge personal greed, which is usually a precursor of malicious intent and fraudulent thinking? Avarice pushes a person to engage in acts like diversion of funds or conducting risky trades.

Decades ago, as a cocky, first-time director, Gopal was disconcerted to find out about a significant financial misdemeanour by a subordinate. The offence was career-damaging and would hurt the subordinate's leadership position. More importantly, it could dent the company's reputation, if discovered. Gopal intuitively sought corporate support from the company CEO and chief financial officer (CFO), who sensed his vulnerable

---

[8]Ariely, Dan, *Predictably Irrational: The Hidden Forces that Shape Our Decisions*, HarperCollins, 2019.

state. Fortunately, over the next few months, the company helped Gopal clear the financial mess. Embarrassed about the financial blunder that happened under his supervision, Gopal was spared the humiliation of appearing incompetent before a wider audience. A little courage and moral forthrightness saved the day.

Over the years, Gopal's vast experience and considerable expertise gained by navigating corporate culture, and overseeing corporate activities and performances from a vantage position on multiple boards have helped him identify some distinct signals that indicate something being amiss and warrant an enquiry.

The Prodromal Test

While prodromal signals are the warnings that precede a mishap, they may not accurately predict a crisis. However, these signs certainly point to a failure brewing. We have designed a simple, but not perfect, test to evaluate prodromal signals of an impending corporate crisis. The test result is cautionary and indicative of the required level of alertness. The test has been validated by applying it to 15 established corporate failures. Although no single response is a complete prodrome, the result, when considered collectively, is meaningful and can indicate a lurking malaise.

Assign 1 point every time you respond 'yes' and 0 points every time you respond 'no' to the questions below.

1. The firm is portrayed as being the handiwork of a single genius, who is highly profiled.
2, The entrepreneur and his firm work hard to remain highly prominent in public.
3. The entrepreneur appears to have access to people in high places, and these connections are leveraged for the firm's benefit.

4. The firm consistently delivers unbelievably good results, out of line with other similar businesses.

5. The entrepreneur seems adept at exploiting weaknesses in the law or 'reinterprets' the implementation of regulations.

6. The entrepreneur is excessively impatient about growth and appears to be greedy for personal wealth accumulation.

7. The firm run by the entrepreneur borrows heavily, often running up unwieldy and ballooning debt obligations.

8. Intelligent investors find it difficult to understand the interconnected web of subsidiaries and associates of the firm, and its consequent accounts.

9. The firm is not acclaimed for great practices, for example, an effective whistle-blower scheme. The governance of the firm is opaque and independent directors appear friendly/ grateful to the entrepreneur/chairman.

10. The auditor is either an unknown entity or a well-known firm, which strives to maintain good relations with the company.

11. There is persistent water-cooler talk about the use of unusual means, though, in the absence of proof, everyone maintains silence.

12. The entrepreneur and/or his family have ostentatious lifestyles—for example, hobnobbing with celebrities—that attract media reportage.

13. The line between the firm's wealth and personal wealth seems to be thin.

14. In interviews, the entrepreneur displays personal panache and bravado while also quoting modest family origins, spirituality or a charitable spirit for society and community.

15. If there is negative reportage, the entrepreneur appears to be shocked and hurt, exhibiting severe denial.

Table 1: How to Interpret the Test Results

Score	Meaning	Comment/suggestion
10–15	Dangerous and dodgy governance	Please reconsider your board position if you are a director
6–9	Average governance	Approach it like most companies but be observant and cautious
1–5	Some imperfections in governance, but within acceptable limits	Help the company improve

Before administering the test and looking for specific signals that may be symptomatic of an imminent crisis, let's understand why people—especially those in responsible corporate positions—misbehave in the first place.

3

Misbehaviour: Understanding Boardroom Dynamics

When Kingfisher Airlines went bankrupt and Vijay Mallya absconded to foreign shores, the post-mortem investigation opened a Pandora's box. Misgovernance and financial mismanagement brought down the luxury airline after seven operational years, with accumulated losses of more than ₹9,000 crore. It was alleged that the owner cheated banks by over-invoicing and diverted the loan money from banks to tax havens overseas through dummy directors and shell companies.[9] The Serious Fraud Investigation Office (SFIO) also found that the owner 'roped in persons of eminence' to make banks 'believe that corporate governance was not lax'.[10]

---

[9]Ghunawat, Virendrasingh, 'Vijay Mallya Used Kingfisher Airlines to Launder Rs 9990 Crore, Reveals ED Chargesheet', *India Today*, 21 June 2008, https://tinyurl.com/2he9bvsb. Accessed on 22 June 2023.

[10]Narayan, Khushboo, 'Kingfisher Struck Deals with Board Directors: SFIO Report', *The Indian Express*, 8 October 2017, https://tinyurl.com/2ad6h9cz. Accessed on 22 June 2023.

This case is an excellent example of the enormous invisible pressure on directors who may inadvertently become party to promoters' misbehaviour. Boardrooms are, after all, constituted by humans who are susceptible to misbehaviour. These can range from outright fraud, light internal audits, unqualified board members to inconsistent delegation of duties leading to governance failures.

These failures usually relate to three levels of governance: the structure of the board, the governance culture and the governance behaviour. There are certain key cognitive biases that can impede the effective functioning of boards at these three levels. These biases influence our thinking unknowingly. This tendency can be traced back to the propensity of the human brain to simplify information through a filter of personal experience and preferences. For instance, some people believe that good-looking people are smart or that confident politicians are competent. On a positive note, there are prescribed mechanisms to help recognize these biases and work towards mitigating them, which all directors must learn to do.

This chapter discusses the three levels of governance, breaks down the biases that impede them and prescribes mechanisms to mitigate them.

Governance Structure

Much of the discussion on boardroom governance has to do with governance structure. Therefore, concerns about the independence of the directors, their skill sets and competencies, their backgrounds and their diversity are crucial elements related to governance structure. However, these components of governance mostly miss the human factor or have the authority bias that probably exacerbates concerns in boardrooms.

Authority Bias and Long Tenures

The authority bias refers to the human proclivity to defer to authority in all situations, more so in boardrooms, which can have serious consequences for the company, its stakeholders and even the nation.

Imagine a corporate board comprising 'independent directors' as required legally. However, these directors are connected with the owner or promoter through various business or social relationships. Alternatively, their board appointments may have happened through word of mouth or through fellow board members' recommendations. Such boards consist of people who agree with or are known to and reliable for the promoters, thereby representing a safe proposition for them. However, such boards become breeding grounds for obedience and lack of dissent, owing to a clear manifestation of an authoritarian figure. This can potentially compromise the system of direction and control of the organization and lead to misbehaviour.

Take the case of Victoria's Secret, the American lingerie, clothing and beauty retailer. The company found itself in the eye of a storm due to several issues, including some related to its governance structure, especially after 2016. In an open letter to 81-year-old Leslie Wexner (the company CEO and chairman of the board of Victoria's Secret), an activist investor group by the name Barrington Capital, pointed to issues stemming from the lack of independence of and diversity in the board.[11] From the 12 directors on the board, eight were found to have strong social and professional ties with Wexner and his wife, as well as with each other, either through the community in Columbus, Ohio, where the company was headquartered, or through the Ohio State

---

[11]Haigh, Marilyn, 'Investor asks L Brands to Separate Victoria's Secret, Bath & Body Works', *CNBC Markets*, 5 March 2019, https://tinyurl.com/kftazc6m. Accessed on 4 July 2023.

University—home to the Wexner Centre for the Arts and the Wexner Medical Centre. The activist group also questioned the actual independence of these eight 'independent' directors. The Barrington Group also raised vexatious concerns over long-serving board members and forced the company to make some changes.

The authority bias gets concretized due to long tenures of board members which erodes their actual independence from the owners or promoters. In case of Victoria's Secret, three directors had tenures lasting more than 36 years. These members included David Kollat (the chair of the compensation committee and a former company executive, who served as a director for over 42 years) and Allan R. Tessler (the lead independent director, chair of the nominating and governance committee who served as a director for over 31 years). Barrington Capital also noted that the company lacked 'directors with a diversity of backgrounds, skills and perspectives sufficient to meet the strategic needs of the company'.[12]

Reimagining Board Diversity

Diversity in the company board is another key area of concern related to governance structure. With corporate boards being dominated by a specific gender, the authority bias often leads to a gender bias in addition to other cognitive biases resulting in a lack of inclusion. Prior to 2019, the Victoria's Secret board was blatantly falling short on inclusion and diversity. Nine of the 12 directors were men, despite the company catering largely to a female target segment. In terms of age, the median age of the board members was 71 years while their average age was 70. In June 2021, compelled to reform, L Brands, the parent company of Victoria's Secret, announced that the new board would comprise

---

[12]Cheng, Andria, 'As Victoria's Secret Scuffles, Activist Investor Says Bath & Body Works May Be Better Off On Its Own', *Forbes*, 5 March 2019, https://tinyurl.com/2p84k9bp. Accessed on 6 July 2023.

of seven directors—six of whom were independent and women. This included the chair of the board.

Corporate boards should be sufficiently diverse in terms of age and professional experience, besides gender, to ensure sound strategic and operational decisions. A diverse board has the benefit of a wide range of perspectives that each member brings to the table, thereby facilitating a greater understanding of the customer base and the environment in which the company operates. Such enhanced understanding of users helps the board explore new opportunities for innovation, which ultimately adds value to the business.

In 2014, Walmart considered the technical and digital expertise of 30-year-old Kevin Systrom, former CEO and co-founder of Instagram, as invaluable to its own business when it appointed him to its board of directors. Systrom's skills could help the 52-year-old company connect better with its customers by moving beyond conventional channels to deploying new capabilities through e-commerce and mobile channels.

Diversity, however, has to be interpreted correctly. As Russell Reynolds Associates point out:

> This homogeneity (of the Board) can be a hindrance in an increasingly dynamic environment. As globalization, the rapid deployment of technology, an increasing need for risk management and the shifting demographics of workforces made businesses much more complex, boards began to broaden their composition. But diversity for its own sake falls short of both the need and the opportunity. An evolution is under way, and boards now are beginning to realize that it is the breadth of perspective, not the mere inclusion of various diverse traits, that benefits the organization.[13]

---

[13] *Different is Better—Why Diversity Matters in the Boardroom*, Russell Reynolds Associates, 2009, https://tinyurl.com/2c7hepak. Accessed on 22 June 2023.

Recently, as a best practice, Fortune 250 boards have been including many women directors from non-business sectors, including government service, academia, non-profits and the legal profession. It is an acknowledged fact that women board members bring a particular attitude—being financially risk averse and less overconfident than men—that prevents organizations from taking on high-risk projects. Women are also seen as more trustworthy and collaborative, which can positively impact board dynamics.[14]

Board diversity plays a key role in the behaviour dynamics underlying corporate governance. It may manifest as three broad archetypes that impact the board's effectiveness in terms of control, strategy building and resource allocation, and can result in the formation of sub-groups and herd mentality. These biases can hamper board functioning. These archetypes have been discussed below.

Heterogeneity archetype: When diversity on a board is based on the variety or heterogeneity archetype, there could be stark differences in the knowledge and experience of board members. This could lead to the formation of coalitions and adversarial behaviour.

Separation archetype: This archetype of diversity could present itself in the form of differences in position or opinion among board members coming from differences in attitudes and values. It can further manifest as instances of favouritism and discrimination that prevent the board from discharging its statutory functions.

Disparity archetype: This archetype reflects differences in pay, status symbols or other valued social assets and resources among

---

[14]Orsagh, Matt, 'The Current Status of Women on Boards in 2016: A Global Roundup', *Market Integrity Insights*, 7 October 2016, https://tinyurl.com/4hb9x9pt. Accessed on 4 July 2023.

board members. In this situation, few or even just one member may be significantly more privileged than others.[15]

Boards impacted by such unseen archetypes and undercurrents cannot be effective.

Governance Culture

Culture is an ambiguous and intangible concept with varied meanings for different people. You can sense it and even feel it, but you cannot see it.

Governance culture refers to the culture fostered by the power dynamics invisibly playing out in the boardroom. Such culture comprises the unspoken and unwritten norms, which may not be explicitly articulated. The governance culture may be hierarchical, driven by the presence of a strong leader, leading to an authority bias. It may be highly bureaucratic, where decision-making is based on clear rules and policies. There may also be a culture that brings a relaxed and casual approach, due to the close relations between the directors. There could also be boards that emphasize processes and other specific outcomes.

A 2015 report by Grant Thornton set out culture as the cornerstone of good governance. At the same time, it struck a cautionary note, stating: 'It can be too intangible to mandate action [...] [As such] boards should work proactively with business management teams to foster a corporate culture of effective governance.'[16] Ideally, the board should take responsibility for deciding on strategy and provide direction while maintaining an even equation with the management to implement that strategy.

---

[15]Kaczmarek, S., 'Rethinking Board Diversity with the Behavioural Theory of Corporate Governance: Opportunities and Challenges for Advances in Theorising', *Journal of Management & Governance*, Vol. 21, 2017, pp. 879–906.

[16]'Corporate Governance: The Tone from the Top', *Grant Thornton*, 2015, https://tinyurl.com/34a8puje. Accessed on 22 June 2023.

However, the specific cognitive biases operating within the board may make the fostering of an effective corporate culture difficult.

Group Think Bias

The effectiveness of the board lies in reaching a consensus through discussions, where members can openly share their views, resolve opposing views and lay down individual preferences for the greater good of the organization. However, the group think bias or herd mentality invisibly dominating the board may make this ideal difficult to attain. The group think bias is a significant cognitive bias, other than the authority bias, that may impact major board decisions. It may lead to board decisions being influenced by a critical mass of loud and vocal leaders, whose opinions and decisions are followed by the group for the sake of being accepted. Typically, the board may be willing to go along with the views of its male, long-tenured directors. These may include those with an imposing stature, a baritone voice, the most educated ones or even those with long-flowy beards and the appearance of being wise.

Boardroom dynamics often comprise power asymmetries, with hubristic leaders and a culture that discourages dissent and suppresses criticism leading to subservient boards. At the heart of any robust corporate mechanism lies independent reasoning, which can manifest in the form of dissent. However, corporate history across the world attests to the fact that they have been surprisingly silent despite being aware that everything is not right within. Humans' intrinsic 'loyalty' response has been used to explain the absence of dissent or why there are no key disagreements. How do people resolve the inner tension between following the voice of authority and adhering to what they believe to be true?

In 1961, Yale psychologist Stanley Milgram conducted the Milgram experiments to study how humans resolve the conflict between obedience to authority and/or personal conscience. He was trying to answer the questions: Were Otto Adolf Eichmann—a Nazi Party official and one of the main organizers of the Holocaust—and his accomplices, merely following orders during the German Holocaust? While committing the crimes that they did, were they merely being obedient to the authority of Adolf Hitler?

The experiments, conducted by an authority, dressed in a coat to reaffirm his power, studied the 'effect of punishment on learning and memory'[17] and highlighted the human tendency to obey directions when the authority is perceived as legitimate. This happens even when obedience means administering an electric shock to hurt another subject![18] The presence of a counter authority questioning the first's decisions, however, led to the results being significantly muted. Milgram concluded that people obey either out of fear or out of a desire to appear cooperative, even when acting against their own better judgement and desire.

Such bias to obey perceived authority often plays out on corporate boards too. In fact, it may get further accentuated by the group think bias and lead a board to reach a consensus without critical reasoning for fear of upsetting the apple cart.

A study, conducted in 2021, analysed the manifestation of such group think in decision-making by conducting a hidden profile experiment. Its participants were unaware that they had to coordinate with other members of the group and pool their information to reach the optimal choice.[19] Key bits of information

---

[17]'Milgram Experiment', *Britannica*, https://tinyurl.com/mpn7uvd. Accessed on 4 July 2023.

[18]Macleod, Saul, 'The Milgram Shock Experiment: Summary, Results, & Ethics', *Simply Psychology*, 2017, https://tinyurl.com/54drft9c. Accessed on 22 June 2023.

[19]Coffeng, T., et al., 'Quality of Group Decisions by Board Members: A Hidden-Profile Experiment', *Management Decision*, Vol. 59, No. 13, 2021, pp. 38–55, https://tinyurl.com/mvzs57nd. Accessed on 22 June 2023.

were asymmetrically shared among group members to mimic actual boards, where members have access to diverse information sources. Thus, group members had to come together and share such complementary information to reach high-quality decisions.

The outcome of the experiment was intended to shed light on whether it was possible for companies to benefit from the skills of diverse professionals, especially those who were on the board for the specialist information they possessed individually. It would confirm if the board succumbed to the group think bias and how that affected decision-making.

Imagine a jigsaw puzzle, with different members possessing different pieces. Unless the group gets together, it is impossible to put the entire puzzle together. Thus, the hidden profile paradigm entails that the best decision alternative is 'hidden' and needs to be discovered by sharing all asymmetrically distributed information.

Group Confirmation Bias

The hidden profile experiment highlighted another common bias that operates at both the individual and group levels—the confirmation bias. It is people's tendency to process information by looking for, or interpreting, information that is consistent with their existing beliefs.

At the individual level, people working with a confirmation bias tend to stick to their initial preferences, based on prior experiences or previously acquired information, even when it might be suboptimal. At the group level, the initial majority preference is taken as the final group decision, as it leads to a quicker resolution. Such group think not only leads to poor-quality decisions but also misleads group members into being highly confident about and satisfied with their decisions, while being mostly unaware of their operational biases.

These experiments imply that a desirable culture for better

governance in the corporate context is one where board members can discharge their duties correctly, without feeling the need to prioritize group cohesion or pressured to agree with others. It is, however, challenging to create such a culture especially when board members have known each other and worked together for a long time and prefer to avoid being perceived as dissenters. Interestingly, on corporate boards, women tend to reduce group think and its associated bias, as they bring different norms, beliefs, behaviours and perspectives to the table. This, in turn, impacts the governance behaviour on the board.[20]

Governance Behaviour

Board behaviours are primarily influenced by the composition of the board. This includes the directors' combined skills, competencies and experience in addition to their personal behavioural style and how it aligns with the character and competence of the directors providing strategic direction to the organization. At the time of nomination of new members, the committee should look beyond factors like qualifications and experience, and go in favour of those who possess critical soft skills like self-esteem, self-management, integrity, honesty, interpersonal skills, emotional maturity, a sense of servant leadership and the ability to work with other cultures and genders. However, this is easier said than done, particularly when several cognitive biases keep playing out unconsciously. Some of the common biases to look out for have been discussed below.

---

[20]Dang, Rey, and Linh-Chi Vo, 'Women on Corporate Boards of Directors: Theories, Facts and Analysis', *Board Directors and Corporate Social Responsibility*, Sabri Boubaker and Duc Khuong Nguyen (eds.), Palgrave Macmillan Books, 2012, pp. 3–21.

Status Quo Bias

Most humans are naturally resistant to change and board members are no exception—they too exhibit a status quo bias. This implies a preference for an existing set of norms and values that are familiar. Thus, boards tend to overvalue what they know and hesitate to support initiatives involving substantial change, simply because there are too many risks associated with the unknown. For instance, while directors may support diversity, it is debatable how many would welcome dramatic changes in the functioning of the board. A board's reluctance to embrace new strategies and ideas, like digitization due to a lack of digital savvy or even hesitation to include women members on the board, reflects the status quo bias.

Some reputed international companies have demonstrated such resistance for change. The 2020 Global Board Diversity Tracker, developed by the leadership advisory firm Egon Zehnder, reported that of the 44 countries studied, 25—including some of the world's largest economies such as China, Brazil, Germany and the US—were still home to large companies with no women on their boards. In fact, it is surprising that India, which was among the list of countries studied, fared fairly well on the diversity factor, with major companies having at least one woman on their board in 2018.[21]

Overconfidence Bias

Boards may also be driven by the overconfidence bias, a cognitive bias where people have an inflated perception of their skills and abilities. The overconfidence bias can lead to glaring discrepancies between perception and reality as brought to fore by a 2015 Grant Thornton study. The report revealed that boards worldwide are

---

[21]'2020 Global Board Diversity Tracker', *Egon Zehnder*, https://tinyurl.com/2ztzp4ba. Accessed on 22 June 2023.

predominantly male with only one-sixth of the directors globally being women. Yet, more than two-thirds of the business leaders believed that they have done a marvellous job of promoting diversity.[22]

Overconfidence is also a common psychological bias among individuals. However, in boardrooms, it becomes collective overconfidence in the team's decision-making. Take the case of a merger and acquisition (M&A) decision involving a failing company. The CEO was overconfident about turning the company around, and the board members meekly acquiesced with his opinions, leading to the contagion effect of overconfidence.

The overconfidence bias may lead to limited rationality in the board's decision-making skills, especially in authoritarian companies. It also appears that the board's chairperson may well be the source of the collective overconfidence, and unduly influences the board through the authority bias.

The chairperson's psychological bias in the boardroom is magnified 2.7 times for the board of directors.[23] This leads to the contagion effect and a collective misjudgement of risks and returns from particular investment decisions, which can impact the business adversely. Research indicates that traditional corporate governance mechanisms cannot address the contagion of overconfidence emanating from the chairperson. It can only be mitigated through better communication and a greater number of board meetings and discussions.[24]

---

[22]*Corporate Governance: The Tone from the Top*, Grant Thornton International Ltd, 2015, https://tinyurl.com/34a8puje. Accessed on 22 June 2023.

[23]'2020 Global Board Diversity Tracker', *Egon Zehnder*, https://tinyurl.com/2ztzp4ba. Accessed on 22 June 2023.

[24]Liang, Chao, Bai Liu, and Yin-Che Weng, 'Blind Following in the Boardroom: Evidence of Overconfidence Contagion in Chinese Listed Companies', *Borsa Istanbul Review*, Vol. 22, No. 3, 2022, pp. 594–606.

Sunk Cost Bias

To ensure good governance, boards must be able to make well-discussed yet swift decisions, especially when confronted with a previous decision gone wrong. In such situations, members on most boards may be susceptible to the sunk cost bias where they may be unwilling to abandon initiatives or ideas on which they have invested time, money and effort, even if they are no longer valid. For example, a company may proceed with a merger and acquisition (M&A) transaction, even though there may be clear indications that it is not worthwhile due to unanticipated legal issues or changes in the business environment. However, having spent months in the planning and preparations for the deal to go through, the board may hesitate to give up on it.

Board members and directors must closely examine some of these covertly visible cognitive biases and practices at work in their respective boards. Table 2 summarizes the biases operating in the boardroom.

Table 2: Signs and Checks for Boardroom Cognitive Biases

Type of Bias	Practice	Mitigatory Checks
Authority bias	There is a clear authority figure—like the owner, promoter or board leader—the board defers to.	Board leaders should rein in their urge to act as leaders in all matters and encourage diverse opinions.
	The directors or board members do not voice their opinions aloud and instead get into side discussions among themselves.	Each director's view on every issue should be actively solicited. Each director should be required to express his opinion on a particular issue.

Type of Bias	Practice	Mitigatory Checks
	One person controls the conversation and has the last word on all board matters.	The authority figure or board leader should hold back his opinion and hear everyone else's views so that his opinions do not influence the others.
	The directors explicitly or implicitly admit that their concerns or opinions do not matter, possibly because they are less experienced.	All directors should be given training in all specialized areas pertaining to corporate governance so that they can deliberate and provide opinions on all these topics.
Group think bias	Controversial topics are not brought to the board. The board leader, working with the CEO or a few members of the board, may decide on them.	Get each director to provide their view separately before the view of the board leader is known, especially on controversial issues.
	Most meetings end with the directors' consensus on the issues discussed. To this end, the leader proposes nodding in agreement.	Bring in outsiders as directors who are known for their independent views and who may not succumb to corporate niceties.
	Dissent is not encouraged. Directors who question or criticize a decision are marginalized or not considered for re-election.	Bring in outside experts or advisors who can have dissenting views.

Type of Bias	Practice	Mitigatory Checks
	Board materials are either presented with little time to review them or are not discussed at all.	Get the company management to present all relevant material to the board on time.
	Board members loathe changing strategies despite changing business environment.	Get board members to see how the company would have done had they developed a different strategy.
	There is no long-term succession plan for board members beyond the one triggered by directors' retirements.	Have specific terms for board members.
Status quo bias	There are a large number of long-serving directors on the board.	Have specific terms for board members.
	There is no periodic rotation of committee chairs.	Have clear terms for committee chairs.
	The board does not question the company management on poor performance.	Initiate and nurture constructive questioning.

Type of Bias	Practice	Mitigatory Checks
Confirmatory bias	Many board members come from similar backgrounds.	Emphasize on the diversity in the room or ask board members to take hypothetical, dissenting views.
	Board members refer to past experiences rather than looking at current evidence and facts during decision-making.	Ask the audit team or other teams to provide data-based challenges to the prevailing view.

Source: Adapted from *Unpacking Board Culture: How Behavioral Psychology Might Explain What's Holding Boards Back*, PwC, February 2022, https://tinyurl.com/nn7eanhx. Accessed on 22 June 2023.

While much of this misbehaviour is common across all kinds of companies, family-led companies pose distinct governance challenges due to their peculiar organizational structures. There is an overlap between the family, the business and ownership sub-systems in such companies. The following chapter discusses the governance challenges of promoter-led companies and their unique biases.

4

Governance of PDCs and
Family Firms

Promoter driven companies (PDCs) or family firms are businesses where promoters or the controlling family own the majority share of company stock, which gives them the power to influence the board. While PDCs are neither good nor bad per se, most of them are afflicted by misgovernance stemming from biases and the clout and authority that many founders enjoy.

The power PDCs can exercise has been increasing. PDCs today constitute 75 per cent of Indian stock exchanges' market capitalization, compared to less than 33 per cent market capitalization about 30 years ago.[25] PDCs have excelled in performance and profits. Their shares have outperformed others by 115 per cent over the last decade. According to the Bombay Stock Exchange (BSE), the operating profits of family-owned businesses on the BSE 500 grew by 13.7 per cent in the last five

[25]Shyam, Ashutosh, 'The "Skin Effect" and Business Performance', *The Economic Times*, 1 December 2018, https://tinyurl.com/26phatut. Accessed on 4 July 2023.

years.[26] The issue of corporate governance becomes critical in such PDCs. In fact, PDCs in India have accounted for a significant portion of corporate misgovernance in recent years, from outright frauds to undue enrichment and retired founders imposing their will on boards.

Satyam: Riding the Misgovernance Tiger

Take the case of Satyam Computer Services, and its corporate misgovernance related to falsification of accounts including overstatement of revenues and diversion of funds to related parties. Satyam (which, ironically, means 'truth' in Sanskrit) began as a small firm with 20 employees in 1987. It offered IT and business process outsourcing (BPO) services across various sectors and went on to become the fourth largest IT software exporter in the industry by 1991, after TCS (Tata Consultancy Services), Wipro and Infosys.

By 2008, Satyam had a workforce of over 50,000, with operations in more than 60 countries and its net worth crossed the $2-billion mark. Satyam had a compounded annual growth rate (CAGR) of 40 per cent, operating profits of 21 per cent and witnessed a 300 per cent gain in its stock price during this period.[27] The highly successful firm was recognized as the Leader in Indian Corporate Governance and Accountability and won the Golden Peacock Award for Corporate Leadership and Institutional Excellence in 2008. The organization was named the winner by The World Council for Corporate Governance (WCFCG), with Dr Ola Ullsten, the former prime minister of

---

[26]Ibid.

[27]Almeida, Aron, 'Satyam Scam – The Story of India's Biggest Corporate Fraud!', *Trade Brains*, 21 January 2023, https://tinyurl.com/476swumm. Accessed on 22 June 2023.

Sweden, serving as lead judge.[28] Satyam's founder Ramalinga Raju was also feted with the Ernst and Young's Entrepreneur of the Year award in 2008.

The company seemed to be booming but then the Satyam scam came to light. A series of events unfolded, revealing the nature and extent of the fraud. In late 2008, Satyam's board decided to take over Maytas, a real estate company owned by Raju. However, shareholders rejected Satyam's decision to take over Maytas in less than 12 hours. This impacted the company's stock price. On 23 December 2008, the World Bank accused Satyam of providing improper benefits to its staff and failing to maintain the documentation to support the fees charged for its subcontractors. The World Bank then barred Satyam from conducting business with any of its direct contacts for a period of eight years. While Satyam challenged the World Bank's decision, Raju resigned on 7 January 2009, confessing that he had manipulated accounts worth ₹7,000 crores.[29]

In the Quicksand of a Fraud

Satyam's rot, manifesting in the form of board misgovernance, happened over a decade. Conspiring with the company's global head for internal audit since 1999, Raju had been manipulating results and inflating revenues and quarterly profits to meet analyst expectations. He created several bank statements on his personal computer, thus inflating the balance sheet with cash that simply did not exist. The internal audit head inflated revenue by creating fake customer identities and bogus invoices.

---

[28]'Satyam Receives Golden Peacock Global Award for Excellence in Corporate Governance', *Financial Express*, 23 September 2008, https://tinyurl.com/2sjv3e5u. Accessed on 7 July 2023.

[29]Almeida, Aron, 'Satyam Scam – The Story of India's Biggest Corporate Fraud!', *Trade Brains*, 21 January 2023, https://tinyurl.com/476swumm. Accessed on 22 June 2023.

Consequently, the quarterly company results announced on 17 October 2009 overstated revenues by 75 per cent and profits by 97 per cent. Such inflated revenues helped the company boost share prices and gave it easy access to loans. Raju went on to manipulate the system further. He created records for fake employees and withdrew salaries amounting to $3 million every month on their behalf, even as he appropriated the money raised from the US markets. As share prices rose, Raju sold as many of his own shares as possible while holding on to just enough to continue being a part of the company. He made substantial profits at the cost of unsuspecting and genuine investors.[30]

With these fraudulent gains, Raju entered the property business with his real estate company called Maytas. He was aware of the state government's plans to build a metro in Hyderabad, and his strategy was to capitalize on this development by selling real estate when the metro came up. However, his plans went horribly wrong when the real estate sector took a hit during the 2008 recession. There was no chance of Raju bridging the huge gap he had created in Satyam's books through years of financial statement manipulation. Satyam's financial statements contained hugely overstated assets and under-reported liabilities, with nearly $1.04 billion in bank loans and cash that did not exist![31]

Meanwhile, Krishna G. Palepu, a company director at Satyam, received anonymous emails from a whistle-blower—using the alias Joseph Abraham—exposing this fraud. Palepu shared the emails and the concerns raised with another director and with the company auditor, S. Gopalakrishnan, a partner at PwC (PricewaterhouseCoopers International Limited). It was then discovered that the alleged complicity of the auditor lay at the heart of the Satyam scandal.

---

[30]Ibid.
[31]Ibid.

Missing the Signs

Despite auditing Satyam for nine years, PwC had failed to notice 7,561 fake bills.[32] The US bank Merrill Lynch too had the dubious distinction of having been Satyam's principal banking adviser for close to a decade, assisting the company with its US listing, follow-on share sales and rights issues. In December 2009, Satyam hired Merrill Lynch to help explore strategic opportunities—code for helping it find either a partner or a buyer.[33] However, Merrill Lynch terminated its working relationship with Satyam when it discovered financial irregularities—something PwC had not managed in nine years—in just 10 days. Investigations later revealed that PwC was paid twice their regular fees for their services, which probably explained why they had turned a blind eye to the obvious red flags.[34] Even after the whistle-blowing incident at Satyam, PwC and its auditor, S. Gopalakrishnan, assured Palepu that everything was well. They further told Palepu that a presentation would be made before the audit committee to clear any confusion on 29 December 2008.[35]

To avert the impending disaster, Raju prepared for Satyam's takeover of Maytas. He could then explain the discrepancy in the

---

[32]Ibid.

[33]Brooks, L.J., and Dunn, P., *Business & Professional Ethics for Directors, Executives & Accountants*, Cengage Learning, New York, 2014.

[34]Upadhyay, Jayshree P., 'Price Waterhouse Firms Banned for 2 Years Over Satyam Scam: What SEBI Said', *mint*, 11 January 2018, https://tinyurl.com/bd35y7pe. Accessed on 4 July 2023; 'Tribunal Quashes SEBI's Ban on PwC in Satyam Scam', *mint*, 9 September 2019, https://tinyurl.com/5n6dntms. Accessed on 4 July 2023. Initially, SEBI had placed a two-year audit ban order on PwC. Later, the Securities Appellate Tribunal (SAT) overturned SEBI's order and lifted the ban on the grounds that such punitive action was beyond the remit of SEBI. It contended that auditors could only raise concerns when they came across something suspicious and not actively search for suspicious activity. They absolved PwC saying they could not be accused of fraud on the basis of negligent auditing.

[35]The date was later revised to 10 January 2009.

financial statements by showing that the money was utilized to purchase Maytas. The proposal failed when shareholders opposed this purchase. Raju was, thus, forced to take responsibility for the fraud he had perpetrated over a decade. PwC tried to clear its name by asserting that the failure to detect the fraud was due to its reliance on information provided by the management.

The Satyam scam also brought to light the role of independent directors in cases of corporate malfeasance, especially involving PDCs.[36] The list of prominent independent directors at Satyam included a marquee list of academics and industry professionals, including Harvard professor Krishna G. Palepu; 'Father of the Pentium processor' Vinod Dham; former Cabinet Secretary T.R. Prasad; former Indian School of Business dean M.R. Rao; former Indian Institutue Technology (IIT) director V.S. Raju and US-based academic and former Harvard professor Mangalam Srinivasan. The Hyderabad court levied fines on all the independent directors, thereby holding them accountable for the company's actions.

Governance in Family Firms

Corporate governance of family firms and PDCs, like Satyam, can differ significantly from the governance of non-family businesses, especially in terms of the goals pursued. A family firm may seek cohesion and a shared vision within the family. Its governance could be influenced by characteristics typical of family firms— ensuring that the firm is passed over from one generation to another—thereby preserving the family legacy and the dominance of the family in the firm's ownership. Therefore, within family

---

[36]Chatterjee, Dev, 'Satyam Fine Sends Signals to All Independent Directors', *Business Standard*, 11 January 2018, https://tinyurl.com/y99wmztj. Accessed on 22 June 2023.

businesses, informal corporate governance practices may prevail over more formal mechanisms. Unlike large companies, boards in family firms are more likely to be small, informal and passive entities.

The formal definition of corporate governance—'the system by which companies are directed and controlled'[37]—focusses only on formal governance mechanisms. However, informal processes form an integral part of governance. They include trust, altruism, social networks and informal dyadic or group interactions between the CEO and board members.

These softer reciprocal processes, based on clear communication, are considered even more important and effective than formal mechanisms, particularly in the case of family firms. They are a unique example of companies where a professional CEO— probably the only non-family member on the board—and the owners engage in informal, dyadic discussions as part of the firm's governance. Such discussions can help align the board, thereby influencing the content and conduct of the formal board discussions, although it will not replace them. This ensures that the proposals placed before the board in its formal meetings are not challenged and that the decisions of the board remain within the Overton window[38], which is confined to options acceptable to the owners or the chair[39]. The operation of such a window can effectively reduce the number of alternatives proposed, and the differing views expressed in board meetings.

---

[37]Cadbury, A., *Report of the Committee on the Financial Aspects of Corporate Governance*, Gee, London, 1992.

[38]Overton window is an approach to identify the ideas that define the spectrum of acceptability of governmental policies developed by Joseph Lehman of the Mackinac Center for Public Policy. It is named after Joseph P. Overton.

[39]Sievinen, H.M., T. Ikäheimonen and T. Pihkala, 'The Role of Dyadic Interactions Between CEOs, Chairs, and Owners in Family Firm Governance', *Journal of Management & Governance*, Vol. 26, 2021, pp. 223–53.

Information Asymmetry Misleading PDCs

Another issue afflicting PDCs, especially small and medium enterprises (SMEs), is that when they retain a family CEO, the latter's unwillingness to share information with board members (perceived as outsiders) may lead to information asymmetries. It is well-known that family-centred, non-economic goals like family dynasty continuity, retention of family control, altruism etc., predominate decision-making in family-controlled enterprises as opposed to business-centric economic objectives.

An important non-economic goal is related to family altruism, with the family trying to protect the interests of friends and relatives possibly at the expense of the business. With family loyalty coming into play, family-controlled enterprises may decide to hire and retain incompetent employees, offer contracts to cronies to fulfil family obligations or even use the firm's resources in inappropriate ways to placate discontented relatives. Such non-economic goals may involve withholding sensitive and confidential information, especially from board members perceived as outsiders. Such lack of transparency may be considered vital to avoid being challenged and to retain control. Similarly, family members may not like to wash their dirty linen in public and, therefore, may not bring their conflicts to board meetings where outsiders are present. All this leads to an information asymmetry with outside board members of private SMEs receiving inadequate information, which does not augur well for corporate decisions.

In listed firms on the other hand, directors may turn to secondary sources, such as analyst, media and investor reports for information. SMEs lack such publicly available information. In such cases, information non-disclosure becomes a key behavioural factor contributing to misgovernance.

Non-disclosure of key information can affect a board's service engagement in private SMEs. The presence of outside directors in SMEs may not be as beneficial to the board's and the firm's performance because there may be a greater tendency to withhold information from the board in such firms.[40]

Deviant Behaviour

Typically, founders and promoters of family firms are emotionally connected to the company, which makes them obstinate about its functioning. This leads to them taking decisions that go relatively unquestioned. The possibility of promoters seeking to further their personal interest—inimical to the interest of the company—could lead to corporate governance failure, signs of which seem to be getting apparent in the founder-driven start-up, Byjus.

Byju Raveendran set up his eponymous company in 2011. It evolved into a global EdTech giant providing learning solutions for students. By 2022, it was valued at $22 billion. However, recently, it has been in the news for all the wrong reasons. It came under the scanner for being run without a dedicated CFO, which implies concerns about the accuracy of its financial books.

Raveendran's 20-per-cent equity share in the company makes him the largest shareholder while the second largest investor owns less than 10 per cent of the stock. Raveendran is known to run the company with a core inner circle of trusted executives and co-founders. The board, comprising long-standing backers, is perceived as unquestioning and one that allows the CEO to run the company the way he wants.[41]

The company's statutory auditor, Deloitte, raised a red flag

---

[40]Uhlaner, L., (et al.), 'Are Outside Directors on the Small and Medium-Sized Enterprise Board Always Beneficial? Disclosure of Firm-Specific Information in Board-Management Relations as the Missing Mechanism', *Human Relations*, Vol. 74, No. 11, 2021, pp. 1781–819.
[41]Raghavan, Ranjani, 'Byju Raveendran's Moment of Reckoning', *mint*, 4 August 2022. https://tinyurl.com/y239782j. Accessed on 4 July 2023.

over some of the firm's aggressive revenue recognition practices, troublesome lending arrangements and its constant need for cash. The auditor did not sign off the company's financial statements for the financial year 2020–21 until as late as August 2022. The company's deadline for filing returns had ended in December 2021, despite the deadline extensions provided by the government due to the Covid-19 disruption.

Byju's apparently bundled its hardware sales (from memory cards and tablets) with its software sales (from apps and online classes) in its revenue calculations, which, allegedly, may have been done to inflate revenues. Such hardware sales accounted for 63 per cent of its revenue in 2020 with an annual increase of 55 per cent.[42]

Another alleged deviance was the first loss default guarantee (FLDG) that Byju's provided as a third-party guarantor on a loan received by its subsidiary company, WhiteHat Jr. This meant, if its subsidiary defaulted on the loan, Byju's would have to cover the debt on its own books or obtain funding from private investors. This was a risky proposition and raised concerns. Another dubious practice was Byju's partnership with lenders who assisted parents to finance courses for their children, whereby Byjus could book revenues in advance.

Theranos: A False Unicorn

Another fallen unicorn that teetered into the abyss of behavioural misgovernance was the US-based blood-testing start-up, Theranos.

---

[42]Ghatak, Suprio, 'Why Deloitte has not Signed Byju's Financials for 2020-21 Even After 15 Months [CA Suprio Ghatak]', *Compliance Calendar.in*, 20 June 2022, https://tinyurl.com/5dxcp4mt. Accessed on 22 June 2023; Akhil V., "'Consolidation Complete, Filing Financial Results in June": BYJU's Responds to The Ken Report', *CNBC TV18*, 15 June 2022, https://tinyurl.com/y656c8d3. Accessed on 22 June 2023.

The sentencing of its former chief operating officer (COO) Ramesh 'Sunny' Balwani and its founder–CEO Elizabeth Holmes, holds key lessons for start-ups and India Inc. too.

Holmes, a chemical engineering student, once hailed as the 'next Steve Jobs', dropped out of Stanford to start Theranos in 2003 when she was just 19. She promised a blood-testing revolution with her disease-diagnosing Edison Test Device that promised to detect cancer and diabetes with just a tiny spot of the patient's blood. It promised to do so without using needles and at a fraction of the usual cost and time taken by traditional technology. Holmes leveraged her family connections to bring in the initial investors.

The Theranos board eventually comprised several well-known names, such as former US Secretaries of State George Shultz and Henry Kissinger; former US Defence Secretary William Perry; and a former CEO of Wells Fargo Richard Kovacevich, along with former US Navy admirals and senior defence personnel. Holmes' need to put together such a board is not surprising, given that the company planned to sell its blood-testing devices to the military.

Investor Gullibility or Celebrity Boards?

By 2010, Theranos had received several rounds of funding. Media mogul Rupert Murdoch led a Series A round of funding as early as 2005, besides others such as Oracle founder Larry Ellison and the US pharmacy and retail chain Walgreens. By 2010, Theranos was valued at $1 billion and had achieved the status of a unicorn.

The world was, therefore, shocked when the company's nanotainer or Edison device proved to be unreliable and failed all tests of accuracy. Following an investigation by the FBI (Federal Bureau of Investigation), the company ceased operations in September 2018. Thousands of employees were laid off. The company's efforts to find a buyer proved fruitless. In January 2022, Holmes was found guilty of fraud and conspiracy. It was revealed that board members were lied to and the company's governance style was riddled with a culture of intimidation and secrecy.

In hindsight, how much of Theranos' unicorn status was the result of investor gullibility and what role did a marquee board play in making this unicorn?

Under the Influence of Biases

Most investors in Theranos were probably driven by loss aversion and a fear of missing out on one of the hot rising stars of Silicon Valley start-ups, especially in the context of the investment that was pouring in from high-profile investors.

Such investments from reputedly hard-nosed businessmen and executives can be explained by drawing on the concept of a 'representativeness heuristic', a mental shortcut we use when compelled to judge the probability of an event. Holmes' status as a college dropout from an Ivy League university after just two semesters probably led investors to overestimate the probability of the Holmes-backed Theranos becoming the next big unicorn.

Investors clearly ignored the fact that the Theranos' technology had never been peer reviewed in medical journals. 'Gullible' investors, thus, seem to have paid scant attention to a statistical base rate—namely the success rate of the new technique. Instead, they displayed a base rate fallacy and the typical human tendency of looking for patterns where there are none, based on the causality bias. The causality bias may have led them to believe that successful start-ups are linked to bright, young, restless minds dropping out of college to create unicorns.

Maybe there was also an overconfidence bias, which caused fund managers and investors to throw caution to the wind due to misleading assessments of their own skills, intellect or talent. What else can explain the fact that the company not only became a unicorn but also reached a peak valuation of $10 billion by 2015 despite Holmes' clear inability to explain

Theranos' technology? In fact, even when she explained this supposed innovation as, 'Chemistry is performed so that a chemical reaction occurs and generates a signal from the chemical interaction with the sample, which is translated into a result, which is then reviewed by certified laboratory personnel,'[43] it failed to make the investors suspicious.

Why did illustrious people fail in their vigilance, refuse to speak up when confronted with damning evidence of failure and continue to back a nefarious company with questionable technology? In light of the biases discussed above, this is a moot question. One of the whistle-blowers in this case, Tyler Shultz (grandson of George Shultz and a Theranos board member) was convinced of wrongdoings in the company within a few months of working there. However, when he raised questions about shoddy quality controls and doctored research, he faced resistance from within his own family. His grandfather chose to ally himself with Holmes and Balwani, leading to a family rift.[44] Similarly, another investor, Tim Draper, continued to be an outspoken defender of Theranos until 2018.[45] Their behaviour demonstrates the operation of a range of biases and social pressures that may have affected their judgement.

Peculiar Biases of PDCs

Certain common thinking patterns prevalent among PDCs underlie the behavioural biases impacting their governance practices. Founders and promoters mostly think of their

[43] Little, Katie, 'This May Be the Quote that Doomed $9 Billion Startup Theranos', *CNBC*, 6 September 2016, https://tinyurl.com/ysj76emn. Accessed on 7 July 2023.

[44] Smith, David, 'Ex-Secretary of State George Shultz Was Besotted By Theranos Fraudster Holmes, Book Says', *The Guardian*, 10 January 2023, https://tinyurl.com/36p9fehr. Accessed on 7 July 2023.

[45] Aiello, Chloe, 'Early Investor Doubles Down on Support for Elizabeth Holmes and Theranos: "She Did a Great Job"', *CNBC*, 10 May 2018, https://tinyurl.com/bderjwe5. Accessed on 7 July 2023.

company as their own. They may draw a thin-line between the company's expenses and their family's personal expenses, leading to the bifurcation bias. This bias pushes them to believe in the superiority of the family's heritage assets and leads them to almost completely trust their family members, firmly believing that there can be no wrongdoing in a centrally-controlled family business. The bifurcation bias also leads to minority shareholders being treated as a nuisance to tolerate. The family business, thus, continues its autocratic style of management, driving transactions that could be termed as corporate malfeasance.

Social Proof Bias

Social proof bias afflicts PDCs where family business managers cite fraud and corruption as the cost of doing business in India, evoking instances of other family businesses in the industry that have thrived on wrongdoing. This bias especially manifests within SMEs as a presumed association bias, which leads to the belief that compliance is a wasteful expense that adds to the company's cost. Additionally, a growth focus leads to family business managers— overtly or covertly—endorsing questionable practices like hiring 'specialist consultants' who can help the family business 'cut unnecessary expenses'.

PDC boards tend to overvalue evidence that supports or confirms their beliefs, like 'it is fine to use questionable practices' or 'we are a small company and, therefore, safely off the radar'. Simultaneously, they also undervalue any information that contradicts and challenges their idea, thus demonstrating a confirmation bias. If combined with the overconfidence bias, family firms may overestimate chances of their misdemeanours not being caught and underestimate the cost of fraud. A PDC may believe that even if fraud is detected, it can always hire agents or third parties to take the blame or pay the penalty and continue business operations.

With the emphasis on regulation increasing, PDCs are gradually transforming. In the changing Indian business landscape, there is a greater demand for PDCs to undertake ethical business and to demonstrate strong corporate governance. Board members, investors, auditors and other stakeholders associated with the governance of start-ups and PDCs—and of large companies as well—must understand the limitations of the traditional approach to corporate governance. Corporate India needs to invest on understanding behavioural corporate governance, since infractions like the ones committed at Theranos, far from being an exception, may turn out to be the rule even as we toast 'Startup India'.

5

Mantras for CEOs and Independent Directors

All business inevitably entails risk and the possibility of failure. When a corporation fails, it is important to distinguish whether an error led to the failure or if it was misconduct and fraudulent misbehaviour by the corporation. An honest failure should not be punished because it is usually contained, and does not have devastating consequences for stakeholders. Failure can be caused by ill-conceived, badly executed or fraudulent decision-making that involves strategic, premeditated deceit. This affects the trust in the company, even the system, and destroys shareholders, lenders and employees. Often, fraud is born when a risk that bets the whole institution goes wrong. These bets are irretrievably dangerous. Since every failure is not a fraud, we should consider the *vichaar* (intent) and the *aachar* (conduct) behind it. A failure is often preceded by erroneous aachar before ill-directed vichaar manifests. Aachar is easier to observe and judge than vichaar.

It is possible to clearly distinguish good governance from bad. When the enterprise is driven by a competent management and effective board processes—like risk reviews and an audit committee that does its job—board members clearly record constructive dissent at meetings. Even the board's decisions are ethical, transparent and directed towards benefitting stakeholders. In such a situation, governance is clearly led by clean intention and conduct. Bad governance is coloured by unfair policies, biases, deceit and corruption. The intent influences the conduct and may be judged, accordingly, in context.

Decoding Aachar and Vichaar

Whether in corporate or public life, errors are inevitable. What you do after the error determines whether it leads to disaster. You may not think you have erred, but others judge the event through a social context and place the blame accordingly.

Though this may be an extreme example, remember that during the Nuremberg trials, those accused of the Nazi Holocaust did not admit to their crimes, but the world judged them for their actions. Likewise, when the International Military Tribunal for the Far East (Tokyo Trials) judged Japanese actions during the Second World War, they found the accused guilty and declared penalties ranging from death to seven years of imprisonment. Such public trials reveal the gap between the someone's aachar and vichaar for which they are then judged. Public judgement can accentuate the failures in companies and make them embarrassing.

In 2001, Ratan Tata was the whistle-blower for the Tata Finance fraud. He immediately admitted the error and then mandated his finance colleague, Ishaat Hussain, to investigate the fraud, review company operations and rescue it. These experiences make one think deeply about what a leader should do when faced with a serious error that has happened on their watch. Not many companies, however, can do this because human biases often interfere with the correct course of action.

Social Context

Dr Elizabeth Kübler Ross observed a five-stage behavioural pattern among life-threatened and terminally ill patients.

1. **Denial** about the onset of the disease.
2. **Anger** arising from the question, 'Why me?'
3. **Negotiation** by blaming others and endlessly discussing alternative solutions.
4. **Depression** stemming from all alternatives looking bad.
5. **Acceptance** leading to positive action.

As you can see, the first four stages take up valuable time before serious action begins.

Let us go back to NASA's HST fiasco, which was declared a leadership failure rather than a technical glitch. The mission leader, Charles J. Pellerin, the much-decorated director of astrophysics, accepted responsibility for this failure and quit NASA. He then joined a business school to research a leadership question: how does one factor social context into management? He and some academics developed a team-building process to help team members understand each other and measure social context.[46]

We do not intend to delve into the details of how social context was sought to be measured in the work done by Pellerin and his academic colleagues. It is sufficient to point out that mature groups of people understand the impact of culture and team climate. They create mechanisms to measure and monitor these soft indicators that practically impact everything and can predict unexpected behaviours.

For example, when Gopal was chairman of Unilever Arabia, one of the mandates of the newly formed Unilever company was

---

[46]Pellerin, Charles J., *How NASA Builds Teams: Mission Critical Soft Skills for Scientists, Engineers, and Project Teams*, Wiley, 2009.

to mount a market assault on the dominant market share of its competitor, P&G, in powder detergents. There was a lot at risk in terms of capital reputation for the company. Gopal realized the newly appointed regional managers were palpably tensed. Could they speak truth to power? Could they share their apprehensions? There was no organized methodology to measure social impact within the company. Gopal travelled widely to meet and interact with the less powerful people in the organization—distributors, retailers, junior sales officers—who expressed their innermost concerns with candour. It was an imprecise but sound form of measuring social impact factors within the organization, and it worked well for the company.

Mantras for CEOs

Having worked for decades in a variety of boardroom positions— including executive director, non-executive director, independent and non-independent director in Indian and foreign corporations— Gopal has seen a lot, if not everything. Here are some mantras he has learnt and used over the years that you may find helpful.

Mantra 1: Directors Seek 'Effective' Solutions While Executives Seek 'Efficient' Solutions

Efficiency and effectiveness are not the same. Efficiency is about maximizing results with the least effort. For example, running fast on level ground without loss of energy by wearing good quality running shoes. Effectiveness is about achieving a goal even if the progress is slow. For example, climbing a steep mountain path without slipping on the rocks.

Successful executives are trained to seek *efficient* solutions. This involves going from one position to another in a straight line. Successful board directors learn to seek *effectiveness*, which may, in many cases, necessitate a circumlocutory strategy. An efficient organization may prescribe a code that involves executives working on projects they are familiar with. In contrast, in an effective organization, executives may get to work on projects that they initially do not comprehend.

Efficient organizations tend to plan in detail. They tend to review actions against this plan or impose processes, responsibilities or deadlines according to it, in addition to providing the resources to accomplish these tasks. On the other hand, an effective organization does not map out the way forward in great detail; it tries new strategies and flexibly adjusts the plan. It expects progress not completion, as it is able to innovate new options and invest appropriately rather than continually adding more resources.

Common house flies are the perfect analogy for efficient versus effective working styles. Flies move in circles rather than flying on a straight path. So, their flight path is effective, though not efficient, because they have compound eyes—about 4,000 immobile, fixed vision crystalline eyes on both sides of their faces—unlike humans, who have simple eyes. Flies assess their distance from their destination, make a move, measure the distance again, readjust their bodies and repeat this process until they reach their destination. The absence of sharp but simple vision prevents them from moving in a straight line, which is the efficient path. Board members facing unpredictable possibilities and outcomes from a project would do well to emulate the effectiveness of common houseflies.

Like the eye of a fly, the 'eye' of an effective organization does not have sharp but simple vision to guide itself forward in a straight line. Instead, the people working for an organization are encouraged to be its 'compound eyes' by thinking for themselves, thereby promoting a diversity of views. An effective organization is the sum of these diverse viewpoints. However, differing views can lead to different agendas, and these can naturally cause great conflict among people and sour human relationships.

While certain kinds of organizational problems need to be

solved efficiently and scientifically, some complex problems need effective solutions. For example, how can the workers and the labour union be persuaded to accept a new wage accord for the long-term benefit of workers and the company? This is a complex problem that needs an effective solution. On the other hand, an issue like 'how can machine productivity be improved from X to Y level?' can have an efficient solution.

Furthermore, people in the organization may not express their views genuinely in formal meetings. If the views expressed by them in meetings are different from their real perception, the complexity of the issue increases. Here, one has to overcome human suspicion, resistance to innovation, lack of trust among workers and the history of worker relationships. Complex problems are not easy to solve efficiently, and need to be handled effectively.

Thus, all organizations have a complex agenda—a compound eye. And, in the end, it is not about whether a compound eye is good or bad, it is just that it is different from a simple eye.

Mantra 2: Learn to Listen

Successful business executives are usually poor listeners. For instance, everyone believes they know how to breathe, but a yoga instructor can swiftly demonstrate that you lack the correct breathing technique. It is so with listening too. However, unlike speaking or presentation skills, there is no course for being a good listener.

Bruno Kahne, a consultant who researched the communication habits of deaf people, uses sign language to 'listen', which makes for a more accurate exchange of ideas. It may be employed by people to improve their communication.[47] He offers five lessons in this regard.

---

[47]Kahne, Bruno, 'Lessons of Silence', *Strategy + Business*, 22 May 2008, https://tinyurl.com/2dyawjr2. Accessed on 17 July 2023.

1. **Look people in the eye:** Unlike those who listen to others while taking notes to remember what was said, deaf people look the speaker in the eye. They absorb and retain more, as they are completely present in the interaction.

2. **Do not interrupt:** In many management situations, there can be multiple conversations happening simultaneously. However, among deaf people, only one person can 'speak' at a time. This rule allows people to reach a consensus more quickly than through a heated and overlapping conversation. In the long term, 'slow' communication is faster.

3. **Keep it simple:** Deaf people are direct and economical about the way they communicate. Due to this, they listen well too.

4. **Request to repeat**: Sign language is evolving faster than the spoken word. With the development of new signs and regional variations in sign language, deaf people do not hesitate to request a clarification.

5. **Be focussed**: Deaf people do not multitask while communicating. They stay away from distractions to focus on the interaction, unlike many directors who are mostly busy on their iPhones during board presentations.

Mantra 3: Treat Directors as Your Senior Friends

Aspiring CEOs typically view the board as a group that endorses their solution, rather than as a body that can assist in finding effective solutions from various alternatives. Directors are usually perceived as an obstacle to be overcome or people who need to be persuaded to agree to a particular solution. This mental model results in behaviours that pitch the board against the management. It would be helpful, instead, to think of directors as a sounding board. They can assist in a situation based on their knowledge and experience. Request their advice to address a problem and learn their perspective. It's best to be respectful of their experience, age and views, even if you do not agree with them on all matters.

Gopal remembers a director who insisted on being addressed by his first name. When he asked why, the director replied, 'If they can't even address me by my first name, how will they ever be able to disagree with me?'

Mantra 4: Directors are Fallible—Get the Best Out of Each One

Every director sitting around the board table has a unique worldview. It might be functional (related to accounting, manufacturing or legal), geographical, experiential (like engineering, software and fast moving consumer goods [FMCG]) or even gender-based, although they may not have the specific expertise about your industry or function. Remember, that is precisely why they are there. Irrespective of whether they are supportive or sceptical, try to understand their perspectives and be respectful either way.

Gopal remembers two experiences of CEOs getting the best out of their directors' while presenting an acquisition proposal to the board. In one case, the board questioned whether the price was too high and if the strategic fit was weak. The CEO gave the perspective some thought and abandoned the plan. In another case, a senior director said to the CEO, 'From what I understand of your business and from what I think you are saying, this may be one of the best acquisition targets in the industry.' The CEO agreed. The director then advised, 'If I were you, I would board a plane and negotiate a purchase price.' That is exactly what the CEO did and the company made a fine acquisition, which has stood the test of time.

Mantra 5: Work Offline with the Alpha Arguers and the Reticent

In every board, 20 per cent of the members are the outliers at each end of the decision-making spectrum while 60 per cent are regular participants. Among these, the alpha arguers hasten to engage on almost every issue at a board meeting. This might be because the engagement demonstrates that they have read the board papers or that they are taking interest in company matters. Nobody wants to take them on. Then, there are the reticent board members who may open their mouth only to sip their tea, but this does not imply that they cannot make a valuable contribution. At one board meeting, a director, usually calm and reserved, became animated when matters relating to manufacturing and safety—both crucial in that industry—were being discussed. He served on committees and helped the management be vigilant on these matters.

Ideally, the chairman should go around the table to encourage participation from everyone. Although this is a delicate process, the management can also attempt to elicit directors' views offline—on the phone, over a drink or a cup of tea. However, he cannot do that as a lobbyist advocating a particular point of view. It must be a genuine effort to assimilate each director's expert view. It may be a demanding exercise but mostly proves to be worth the effort.

Managers are taught to identify and recruit supporters. Politicians are trained to recognize their detractors and carry them along. Aspiring CEOs must acquire both these skills.

Mantra 6: Elicit Views on Long-Term Strategy. Don't Wait for the 'Big Discussion Day'.

There is a fundamental disconnect between directors who like to engage deeply with strategy at a high level and CEOs who enjoy presenting a glorious vision as a grand strategy. Similarly,

CEOs might think they have mentioned every point in the past, but the directors may feel they are hearing it all for the first time. CEOs must use specific nuggets of time to understand each director's perspective on strategy, so that the grand presentation is not wholly novel.

One such CEO, mastered the presentation of the grand strategy. He shaped this strategy based on a discussion with each director before making the formal presentation that incorporated their ideas. This genuine interaction provided insight and made it easier for directors' to finally agree on a course of action.

Mantra 7: Do Not Become Larger than You Are

Successful executives are always at risk of being arrogant, driven by an exaggerated self-image. They overestimate the extent to which they can control events, and underestimate the role of chance and circumstance in their achievements. They have an inflated belief in their personal contribution to the company. As risk-takers, they steer the company towards irresponsible actions that put stakeholders at risk. These behaviours are red flags for directors and a huge detriment for the board. Such executives undermine the service of senior colleagues and gradually exclude them from the decision-making process to eventually gain complete control by setting up a personal staff.

Mantra 8: 'Before Shooting the Arrow of Your Opinion, Dip It in Honey'

This heading comes from an Arabic saying. It suggests that a difference of opinion may be expressed in a positive manner. In the Ramayana, for instance, how did Vibhishana convince an enraged Ravana that killing Hanuman was wrong? Vibhishana first praised Ravana for his accomplishments and then counselled him that killing the messenger would be in violation of diplomatic protocol.

Be careful not to repeatedly express your differing opinion, unless it is a matter of principle, law or propriety. Then, it is your responsibility to offer your views, just as it is incumbent on the director to listen to this differing view.

Mantras for Independent Directors

So far, we have discussed mantras that are suitable for CEOs. Independent directors need a few mantras to work effectively for two principal reasons—for when they engage with the management and because they know less than the management.

Mantra 1: Disagree Without Being Disagreeable

An army officer once faced several unproven charges. Field Marshall S.H.F.J. Manekshaw, former commander-in-chief of the Indian Army, reportedly advised him, 'How can you now lead your men? If I were you, I would shoot myself or resign.'

This is the distinctive nature of dilemmas faced by independent directors. They are expected to lead intellectually and morally without the knowledge and hierarchical authority of the operating managers. Important organizations get engulfed in murky controversies involving CEOs and directors. Just like the wildfires in California, public commentaries can scorch reputations and careers, sometimes legitimately. For example, in the case of YES Bank, the independent NEC resigned on the grounds that he had little faith in the statements and accounts presented by the management led by Rana Kapoor. In the case of Crompton Greaves (CG) Power, on the other hand, the audit committee created conditions for the dismissal of the chairman due to discrepancies in the accounts and board assertions.

Amid such corporate realities, when Gopal had a breakfast meeting with an independent director, the latter posed an intriguing question: 'When an independent director disagrees, is it adequate to merely record his disagreement? Is that independence?'

Governance has two aspects based on knowledge and behaviour. Competent independent directors need to combine both aspects. Only then will their actions be wise. An efficient independent director must be comfortable with the cognitive to deal with matters of knowledge, like products, industry, finance and law. An effective independent director must also act with the behavioural vector of governance. This second aspect, which is cultural, is not sufficiently recognized while framing regulations. Indian governance is modelled on Anglo-Saxon practices rather than local cultural characteristics.

Mantra 2: Understand the Dark Side of Directors' Behaviours

Since behavioural aberrations constitute the prodrome for independent directors to observe and assess emerging signals, they must be sensitive to the dark side of directors' behaviours. The board as a whole must guard itself against the 3Ps: power, passion and predation. The 3Ps constitute the dark side of directors' behaviours while reflecting the motives behind them joining a board.[48]

Power: Directors who seek power do not understand the impact of their behaviour on transparent decision-making and the success of the organization. These directors with low emotional intelligence typically stop at nothing to assume power, resorting to Machiavellian force, manipulation, coercion and even deception to achieve their goals. Such pursuit of power can become abusive, as they may refuse to accept reports at face value or keep questioning it till they are either satisfied or proven right. They may even dominate conversations and resort to cyberbullying after meetings

---

[48]Gilkison, Flora, 'Power, Passion, and Predators in the Boardroom', *Governance New Zealand*, 2013, https://tinyurl.com/kp7ns73w. Accessed on 5 July 2023.

if their preferred course of action is not followed.

It is ironic that the very qualities necessary for becoming an effective leader, like empathy and social skills, may degenerate once an individual is in power. These qualities may be replaced by aggression, self-centredness and impulsiveness. Independent directors must be cognizant of the shadowy uses of power that could compromise the boardroom values of responsibility, trust, social intelligence and cooperation.

Passion: Passion comes into play when there is a sexual relationship within the company, which can damage the quality of decisions taken or subversively influence the board's decision-making. Such influence should normally be governed by the board's code of conduct. Corporates, which usually ignore the transgressions of senior officers of the management leadership group known as chief experience officers, may sometimes take action. An exemplary exception in corporate India was that of Phaneesh Murthy, the IT marketer who was sacked from iGate Corporation for 'not disclosing his relationship with a subordinate'.[49]

The other kind of passion comes into play when a director becomes overly obsessed with another director or even the CEO. Especially when the CEO becomes the object of such passion, the director may transform from being a sidekick to a sycophant or even try to become a clone of the powerful CEO. If the CEO is narcissistic, this passion could be abused to undermine governance. Directors need to be alert for destructive behaviours rooted in such passion, as they are detrimental to the company.

Predation: Predation can take the form of one company stalking another, which is often perceived as a successful strategy. In the boardroom, especially at the time of re-election of board members,

---

[49]Sengupta, Devina, and Sreeradha D. Basu, 'CEOs Have Affairs but Cos Love to Hide Them; More Women in Senior Roles May Change Matters', *Economic Times*, 28 May 2013, https://tinyurl.com/2af2jfef. Accessed on 23 June 2023.

directors wish to promote themselves with voters and may exhibit predatory behaviour vis-à-vis other directors or even the CEO. This further causes unpleasantness and discomfort. These behaviours may result in trust being betrayed and communication becoming fragmented.

Once either of the 3Ps become a part of board culture, it is necessary to restructure the entire board, including the CEO, by ousting them from their positions in certain circumstances.

Mantra 3: Abide by Board Obligations

The board plays the role of protecting the interests of all shareholders and stakeholders. It is a collective obligation. While promoter–directors might inadvertently favour the promoters' interests, independent directors should deeply consider the interests of the retail or minority shareholders.

Independent directors' role is to protect the interest of all shareholders, but especially the interests of minority shareholders. They must, therefore, be advocates with distinctive views that work for the shareholder, yet need not be obtuse crusaders for minority shareholders.

Independent directors must resort to reasoned approaches within the board and among other independent directors to present perspectives from minority shareholders' viewpoint. If this viewpoint is not accepted within the board, it cannot be assumed that the board or management are obstinate. Independent directors must then re-examine the proposed view and the effectiveness of its underlying advocacy. This can be done through a step-by-step approach, which has been discussed below as the 7Ds.

All independent directors must understand the 7Ds that comprise their duty and responsibility. For the board to be effective, independent directors must intuitively follow the 7Ds. However, all too frequently, they fall prey to the group think bias. They follow the herd and fail to act as per the 7Ds.

Independent directors must provide an unbiased perspective and counsel the board of directors. To effectively carry out their duty, independent directors must accede to the 7Ds of their role on the board.

1. **Descry:** Independent directors must develop a point of view by absorbing the subject at hand, listening deeply, observing behaviour and appreciating the context. These are essential, particularly in judging conflict of interest, related party matters and M&As. For example, the fit of a target acquisition may be sound, but its risk profile may be too high for a company's balance sheet.

2. **Debate:** Independent directors must demonstrate the flexibility to consider alternative viewpoints. Independent directors with a single point of view are not of great help. Independent directors with both a point of view and the mental bandwidth to listen to other points of view are more valuable. It is perfectly credible to be persuaded by another viewpoint and defer to the consensus.

3. **Demur:** This is important if two conditions occur simultaneously—first, an independent director has a lurking concern; and second, the subject has adequate materiality for the institution. In such a situation, the independent director must constructively express the discomfort. However, they must not demur so politely and discreetly that the message is lost.

4. **Disagree:** When any dissent is material to the company's business, it must be clearly expressed without fear or favour.

5. **Distance:** If independent directors have advocated a view, and the debate has been professional and constructive, they need to consider whether the subject has enough materiality for the company. In some cases, no great

principle is involved—it is just about one opinion versus another or the management may be seeking bound freedom to experiment. Such proposals can be supported. However, if the proposal has material impact or a matter of principle is involved, independent directors should distance themselves from the decision. How does one do this? In a company, an independent director insisted on his different view being recorded as having 'expressed reservations'—a rather mild way to put it. Another independent director wished for his view to be recorded as 'in disagreement'—a stronger expression of distancing. It depends very much on an independent director's judgement of whether the issue at hand is merely a technicality or an important ethical viewpoint that impacts shareholders.

6. **Depart:** Expressing disagreement or distancing could have unintended consequences. Such dissenting independent directors could be perceived by the management or the promoter group as obstructive. If this circumstance develops, it is time to depart. The departure should be quiet if the disagreements and distancing are not material for the company.

7. **Disclose:** If there is a substantive disagreement or the minority shareholders' interests are being materially affected, independent directors are legally mandated to disclose the reasons for their departure to regulators. If these reasons find their way into the public domain, so be it.

Board members would benefit from adhering to these mantras and the 7Ds for independent directors. This can support them in developing some level of immunity to the power play that typically manifests in boardrooms, as we shall see in the next chapter.

6

Power: Its Manifestation in the Boardroom

Executive power, like narcissistic leadership, is useful when wielded well, but it can be detrimental when not deployed constructively. Thus, one must exercise executive power discerningly. The most incredible impact of power is life-altering change. Positive power, embedded as a leader's keen sense of responsibility, brings authority that is used to influence others. However, there are drawbacks to wielding power, as it can interfere with brain function. Just as an invisible virus in the air can damage the body, power can damage every leader who must, consequently, learn to cope with it and mitigate its arrogance.

The term 'CEO' includes all business leaders with power—promoters, professional CEOs and even the government as promoters of public sector units (PSUs) and public sector boards (PSBs). Power affects all business leaders who need self-awareness and coping strategies. Every leader has experienced the heady effects of power. It was the same with Gopal. Able to reflect dispassionately today, he is thankful that he 'survived' that impact of power.

A CEO can exercise power over employees, associates, boards

and the media. The misuse of power that recently led to the exit of charismatic corporate chieftains worldwide made big news, including leaders from Kingfisher Airlines, ICICI Bank, YES Bank and IL&FS (Infrastructure Leasing & Financial Services) in India; Wirecard, Volkswagen and Audi in Germany; WPP in the UK; and Danske Bank in Denmark.

What went wrong? Are governance regulations lax? What is going on?

Power Damages the Brain

The root cause of CEO misconduct stemming from an abuse of power and position is cultural and psychological. Power is like wealth. The more you chase it, the higher its destructive capacity. Power reduces emotional capacity and damages the leader's brain; it is akin to a strong magnetic field that disturbs the alignment of iron filings, in that it lowers emotional capacity. This manifests as arrogance, pomposity, delusions of heroism, mad pursuit of visibility, disregard of inputs and rudeness, leading to perceptions like 'this is not the same person we knew'. However, the brain may return to normal when the power source is cut off. The nice guy may become kind again!

What exactly happens inside the brain? As a leader gains power, the brain undergoes some physiological and hormonal changes. Toxic traits such as arrogance, volatility, habitual distrust, aloofness and eccentricity start appearing. Several studies have accounted for such modifications, including Professor Sukhvinder Singh Obhi from McMaster, Canada, who studied leaders' brains using a transcranial magnetic stimulation (TMS) machine that utilizes a pulsing magnetic field to study brain activity, thus allowing researchers to track and interpret brain signals.[50]

---

[50]Gopalakrishnan, R., *Crash: Lessons from the Entry and Exit of CEOs*, Penguin Random House India, 2018.

Research has consistently shown that individuals' dominance disposition or implicit power motivation are positively related to baseline testosterone levels, and that situational outcomes can initiate changes. Among women, the hormone estradiol plays a key role in dominance motivation.[51]

A CEO cannot be a person of unsound mind as per the mandate of Section 164 of the Companies Act. On a lighter note, future regulators may require CEOs to undergo a TMS-test with findings duly disclosed in the directors' report before their appointment! It is, however, more probable that their brains may be damaged after becoming CEOs!

Ominous Tales of Leadership Psychopathy

Success can make a leader wealthy, but it can also pose personal and reputational risks. Following the publication of Gopal's book *Crash: Lessons from the Entry and Exit of CEOs*[52], some readers expressed incredulity about how power could actually 'damage' the brain. The causes could stem from the behaviour of the CEO or board, national politics, judicial judgments or even public perception. Unfortunately, even excellent CEOs experience bad luck. Here are some recent incidents, exemplifying these cases, each loaded with a cautionary lesson.

Consider the case of Rajat Gupta's insider trading, which we have mentioned earlier in this book. Despite not gaining anything from the alleged insider trading, he spent years in prison. Similarly, Thomas Middelhoff led the German publishing group, Bertelsmann, with great distinction until 2002, when he was eased

---

[51]Stanton, Steven, J., and Oliver C. Schultheiss. 'The Hormonal Correlates of Implicit Power Motivation', *Journal of Research in Personality*, Vol. 43, No. 5, 2009, doi:10.1016/j.jrp.2009.04.001.
[52]Gopalakrishnan, R., *Crash: Lessons from the Entry and Exit of CEOs*, Penguin Random House India, 2018.

out. Already an international business icon, Middelhoff then joined German retailer, Arcandor, which had fallen on troubled times. However, after some years at Arcandor, he was accused of inappropriate corporate conduct, such as taking private trips on company-chartered aircrafts and lavishly redecorating his office. A judge in an Essen court sentenced him to three years in prison for embezzlement and tax evasion in 2014. Middelhoff was jailed despite his intention to appeal. Released from jail in 2018, he claimed that he had been wrongfully convicted. He did not consider himself to be a criminal, yet he fully accepted his sentence. Eventually, it was revealed that Middelhoff had never wanted to enrich himself, but, regrettably, he had neglected to follow correct procedures because he reportedly claimed to have become out of touch with reality.

Positions of power certainly alter behaviour and trigger hubristic traits that have sent many entrepreneurs to prison. Take the case of Eike Batista, a Brazilian mining tycoon, who was a daring and fabulously successful entrepreneur, in addition to being a symbol of entrepreneurial flair in Brazil. He was well-connected, worked incredibly hard and was the seventh richest person in the world in 2012. The Brazilian President Dilma Rousseff hailed Batista as 'a national pride'.[53] However, it was widely believed that Batista had strong ties with all political parties and, hence, his business empire was sinister. In the shifting political climate after Dilma's regime, Batista was sentenced to 30 years in jail in July 2018. Charged with offering a bribe in exchange for state construction contracts, Batista was allotted an ordinary prison cell with a squat toilet and cold water without recourse to any 'Mallya-esque' tactics.

Zhang Wenzhong, another high-profile and successful promoter of Wumart, a Chinese supermarket chain, was convicted in 2009

---

[53]Gallas, Daniel, 'The Fall of Brazil's Playboy Billionaire', *BBC*, 6 July 2018, https://tinyurl.com/2uvj94x5. Accessed on 23 June 2023.

on charges of fraud, bribery and embezzlement. After 10 years of incarceration, in a different political environment, the Chinese Supreme Court ordered his release with the judgment pronouncing him innocent. Being a high-profile corporate employee and ever-shifting politics make nightmarish bedfellows. *Jinfang* (beware)!

Even the former CEO of Renault and Nissan Carlos Ghosn, spent more time in Japanese jails than he ever could have imagined. Although, all the facts are not clear to the writers, it is disturbing to think that he was held in jail without trial for several weeks.

The mind of a powerful leader must maintain its delicate equilibrium. In his book, *The Wisdom of Psychopaths*[54], psychiatrist Kevin Dutton describes psychopathic behaviour as a leadership hazard. Typically, this psychopathic mindset combines power with ruthlessness, charm and gratification—much like James Bond.

Under intense media scrutiny, a CEO may well be convicted by the public long before the culmination of legal processes. The only solution for CEOs, therefore, is to behave in an exemplary manner, well above the legal prescription.

Leadership Narcissism

Media adulation and self-importance are shimmering mirages in the desert of self-delusion. Every person's perspective is limited because it is shaped by experience, which, of course, only represents a fraction of what is actually at stake. For instance, think of the world's greatest stories and epics. The narratives can vary quite a lot depending on which character's perspective we read them from.

As one of Gopal's bosses used to say, 'Beware of winning an award or appearing on a magazine cover; it may signal the impending decline of a successful career.' He was mortified by fame, which tends to consume even balanced leaders. A CEO

---

[54]Dutton, Kevin, *The Wisdom of Psychopaths*, Arrow Books, 2013.

and all prominent leaders, must learn to withstand the seductive yet temporary spotlight of public attention, which is a major job hazard. There are innumerable articles and books on the elusive subject of leadership narcissism. The *Financial Times* did one such story on the media baron Robert Maxwell.[55] His body was found at sea 30 years ago. The trial and sentencing of his daughter Ghislaine Maxwell, in the Jeffrey Epstein case, had made headlines. Epstein was a financier who had enjoyed close ties with celebrities before he was convicted and sent to prison, where he allegedly died by suicide in 2019. In 2020, Epstein's associate and girlfriend, Ghislaine Maxwell, was also arrested on multiple criminal charges and for abetting his actions.

Skapinker quotes various experts to assert that narcissists usually lack a secure base of love; some have a genetic predisposition to narcissism; many are clever, capable and work prodigiously hard; most of them seek excessive admiration, lack empathy for others and operate with a sense of entitlement.

Independent Directors as the Conscience

Independent directors can play an important role in preventing a power-induced mental modification. Their legal duties apart, independent directors can serve as a conscience for a powerful CEO. Most do this effectively because they are not mere watchdogs, they work to counsel, mentor and persuade CEOs.

If these approaches fail to rein in the CEO, independent directors must threaten and quit, if required, because their loyalty is to the institution not to the leader. That is the wise independent director's dharma. Many boards, including PSB and PSU boards, are dysfunctional because major decisions are taken outside board

---

[55]Skapinker, Michael, 'How to Handle a Narcissist in the Workplace?', *Financial Times*, 25 April 2022, https://tinyurl.com/33hr6rm7. Accessed on 23 June 2023.

meetings. Only the CEO can prevent this and independent directors can be the inner voice helping the CEO stay grounded and humble or even helping him take a step back to see the big picture.

An independent director must have the courage to quit if the CEO does not listen to sage counsel, although such cases are rare. In public affairs, there are some examples of such resignations, like Defence Minister V.P. Singh quitting Rajiv Gandhi's cabinet during the investigation into the Bofors matter. Or the Chairman of SBI R.K. Talwar stepping down during Emergency, when Sanjay Gandhi allegedly tried to bully him into granting loans to people favoured by the government.[56]

Although most independent directors are not aware of the intricacies of the businesses they are on the boards of, over and above facing information asymmetry, they ought to recognize narcissism manifesting through multiple warning signs. Imagine serving on the United Breweries board and not sensing the narcissism! Independent directors who notice these signs have the power to usher change.

J.R.D. Tata once observed that transformers lead with affection. He stated, 'I am one who will make full allowance for a man's character and idiosyncrasies. [...] At times, it involves suppressing yourself. It is painful but necessary. [...] However, when that cup of affection and indulgence becomes empty then it is time to act.'[57] And such action could well mean ousting the CEO.

When CEO and Board Marriages Fail

The functioning of a board is determined by the nature of the relationship among its three constituents—promoter directors, executive directors and independent directors. The evaluation

---

[56]Ninan, T.N., 'T N Ninan: The "Talwar Amendment"', *Business Standard,* 24 January 2013, https://tinyurl.com/2rek765h. Accessed on 5 July 2023.

[57]Lala, R.M., *Beyond the Last Blue Mountain,* Viking, 1992.

of a CEO (used as a surrogate for executive management) is a battle of perception. Boards and remuneration committees hesitate to engage with the behavioural and soft aspects of CEO appraisal. This contributes significantly to board relationships and communications failing.

Gopal was invited to speak on this subject at an event in Boston, in the context of increasing incidences of CEOs being fired or resigning. The question was: can such instances be reduced and, if so, how? Adopting rigorous processes for board functioning—like acquisition evaluations, leadership appraisals, portfolio reviews and so on—obviously helps.

For instance, one year after the American software giant Hewlett Packard (HP) acquired the British software company Autonomy, for approximately $11 billion in 2011, HP had to write off around $9 billion.[58] HP accused Autonomy's founder-CEO Mike Lynch and its CFO Sushovan Hussain of fraudulent accounting that inflated the value of the firm. Considering these circumstances, what do you reckon was the relationship between HP's CEO Léo Apotheker and his board, headed by Chairman Ray Lane? Naturally, Apotheker resigned from the board. This parting occurred just six years after HP's previous CEO Carly Fiorina was asked to leave for her acquisition of Compaq, which was termed the worst merger in 2001.

In 2008, India had a similar case when the Japanese company Daiichi Sankyo acquired Ranbaxy Laboratories by purchasing the brothers Manvinder and Shivinder Singh's equity stake in it. The valuation was based on their due diligence and facts—or judgements based on an interpretation of facts—stated by the management. The deal proved to be a fiasco.

---

[58]Hardy, Quentin, and Michael J. de la Merced, 'Hewlett's Loss: A Folly Unfolds, by the Numbers', *The New York Times*, 20 November 2012, https://tinyurl.com/3za3ua6e. Accessed on 7 July 2023.

Boards often rely on judgements of CEOs. While it is important to judge a CEO's competence based on an objective performance evaluation, is this sufficient? What about judgements? Contrary to corporate governance regulations, there are many subjective and behavioural factors, which make rational evaluation against clear performance metrics somewhat fuzzy. Hence, assessing CEO performance is complex. In our experience, behavioural factors are given low weightage, which creates an illusion that the board's evaluation is objective. The facts prove otherwise.

Key 'chosen' leaders have resigned from the boards of major corporations. Consider the circumstances around the departure of Ramesh Sarin, president at Voltas; Vishal Sikka, managing director and CEO at Infosys; and Suresh Vaswani and Girish Paranjpe, joint CEOs at Wipro. In each of these cases, the boards seem to have been influenced by behavioural issues more than performance factors. Likewise, in the international arena, Chris Viehbacher, CEO at Sanofi, was asked to leave due to his uncommunicative management style. Similarly, G. Richard Thoman, president and CEO at Xerox Corporation, left because he apparently lost the confidence of his colleagues. These instances underline how crucial it is to assess behavioural factors in addition to a metrics-based evaluation.

Behaviour-Based CEO Evaluation

On 25 January 2022, the *Financial Times* published a report about the collapse of two prominent companies—Carillion and Wirecard. Both companies—well-known businesses in their specialized fields—had received glowing reports about the effectiveness and impact of their board processes. However, soon after, shockingly, both companies imploded. It was almost as though the public recognition had been a kiss of death. Incidentally, this seems to happen quite often. Soon after a newspaper or association recognizes the exceptional leadership and governance of a company, unfortunate events follow. Remember Satyam Computers?

In our experience, remuneration committees function diligently. However, they engage more with the hard factors of experience outcomes and focus far less on subtle factors of behaviour or human impact. Under the illusion that their appraisal is objective, some boards justify a large remuneration for an exceptional performance, an action that further fuels scepticism about the CEO evaluation process.

Performance assessment, however, is dominated more by soft, behavioural factors, particularly with an impending divorce between the CEO and the board. Some of these behavioural factors include moving too slowly (for example, the board felt that Tom Flannery, CEO after Jeff Immelt, was restructuring the company too slowly at GE), moving too fast (Chris Viehbacher at Sanofi, where the all-French board felt that Viehbacher was moving away from the core French values of the company), poor relations with investors (Klaus Kleinfeld at Arconic got into an entangled relationship with a financial investor in the company on the grounds that the investor had been spying on CEO Kleinfeld's family) or poor interactions with employees/ associates (Travis Kalanick at Uber who had some incidents of treating employees and associates badly).

The key takeaway from these examples is that CEO evaluations must be influenced by a 'soft, behavioural' component at all times and not only when there are stressed relationships. Boards can candidly discuss behavioural factors only when there is trust among the directors. Essentially, CEO and board marriages demand tactful management of power and ego.

Mitigating Overambitious Tendencies and Foregrounding Humility

A CEO requires steadfast humility to remain grounded through a high-pressure leadership stint. As Sant Kabir Das said, '*Sees utaarai haathai kari, so paisey ghara mahim*[59] (He can lead who gives up his ego by beheading himself).[60] Fortunately, there are more feasible techniques to keep *ahankara* or ego at bay.

The Sanskrit word *charaiveti* is a *sandhi* or portmanteau of *chara eva iti*, which means 'always keep moving'. One becomes humble by practising charaiveti, conscious that every high or low will pass. As the popular nursery rhyme goes,

A wise old owl lived in an oak,
the more he saw, the less he spoke,
the less he spoke, the more he heard,
why are we not all like that wise old owl?

The word 'ambition' originated from the Latin, *ambitionem*, which means 'canvassing', and it used to have a negative connotation. In ancient Greece, ambition was no virtue because it was associated with ambitious politicians who desired glory more than responsibility. Author and thinker, Bill Taylor discussed this in the Harvard Business Review (HBR) of 15 October 2015, lending credence to the widespread notion that humble people cannot be ambitious.[61] Edgar Schein, a leadership professor at MIT, said that this impression is exemplified by newly promoted managers, who responded that now, 'they can tell others what to do'. The reality that 'I am now the boss'

---

[59]Anand, Kulshresth, Swami, कबीरे के दोहे (*Kabir's Couplets*), Alpha Ed, 2020.
[60]Translation by the author.
[61]Taylor, Bill, 'Companies Can't Be Great Unless They've Almost Failed', *Harvard Business Review*, 21 March 2016, https://tinyurl.com/mx26jh2r. Accessed on 5 July 2023.

lies at the root of the problem.[62]

A Nike hoarding in the 1996 Atlanta Olympics asserted, 'You don't win silver, you lose gold.' Fortunately, this widely held belief is incorrect. It is not necessary to be ambitious to succeed in life. Leaders need to think of humility as a tool to be used in service of ambition. While ambition seeks overarching goals, humility acknowledges dependence on others to achieve it. If 'conquest at any cost' is your ambition, unbridled arrogance and ill-treatment of the vanquished is inevitable.

History has borne witness to leaders' ambitions of conquering territories and vanquishing foes. Consider the Roman General Tiberius, who grew morbidly suspicious of everyone, and his ways of asserting power became chilling and monstrous after being crowned emperor. His successor, Caligula, developed paranoia early on after becoming emperor. He started behaving highly erratically. Nero was another emperor whom everybody loved to hate. The list of powerful emperors whose ambition and desire for power made them commit unspeakable atrocities is never ending.

However, there have been some successful exceptions, of course. The Roman General Coriolanus said, 'I do not want the job, but only the honour.'[63] Similarly, Hyder Ali, the defector ruler of Mysore is anecdotally known to have told his son, Tipu Sultan, 'While we may seize a crown, the crown may escape us if we do not trust the love of people.'

So, why are so many leaders arrogant when it is clear that humility is crucial for success? Research indicates that ambition, which drives leadership, is about glory while humility is about

---

[62]Kuppler, Tim, 'Leadership, Humble Inquiry & the State of Culture Work - Edgar Schein', *Human Synergistics International*, 10 March 2014, https://tinyurl.com/yc78fy8b. Accessed on 17 July 2023.

[63]Gopalakrishnan, R., *Crash: Lessons from the Entry and Exit of CEOs*, Penguin Random House India, 2018.

burden and suffering. Do ambition and humility go together? In the traditional view, never the twain shall meet.

Among corporate titans, some leaders are so focussed on ambitious acquisitions that they fail to remain humble and remember that it is part of their job to deliver the benefits of the acquisitions to their shareholders. They burden their successors with a business empire that has been hopelessly extended and financially weakened. We refer to this malaise when we assert that power temporarily damages leaders' brains.

Professor Ian Robertson of Trinity College, Dublin, observed, 'When power is unconstrained by democratic controls or good systems of governance, power holders may show undesirable distortions in judgment, cognition and behaviour.'[64] Strong corporate governance and preventing the blatant or repeated misuse of authority are key strategies to mitigate the negative effects of power.

A Good Behavioural Code

Gopal has been on the boards of Unilever and Tata, both long-surviving practitioners of corporate *ikigai*. From his first-hand experiences on these boards, we understand that sustained business success is hinged on five elements—conservative finance, innovation, continual improvement, relentless adaptation and obsessive corporate governance. Such companies also benefit from the cumulative long-term compounding effect of their good karma or actions. Start-ups must adopt these established pearls of wisdom to succeed.

For instance, 40 years ago, the venture capital (VC) business did not exist. In April 2022, the VC firm Sequoia India published a blog post titled 'Corporate Governance: The Cornerstone of

---

[64]Ibid.

an Enduring Company'.[65] Coming from a pioneer in venture financing, this theme was significant. Unlike most short-lived VC firms, Sequoia—set up in California, US, in 1972—has survived over the decades because, as the company's global CEO Michael Moritz once stated on the *Charlie Rose Show*, 'We are scared of going out of business…We assume that tomorrow won't be like yesterday…We can't be complacent…'[66]

The blog by the Indian branch of Sequoia, set up in 2006, appealed to more participants in the Indian start-up ecosystem to join its pledge for greater governance. The company affirmed that, despite conducting as much due diligence checks as possible, there are constraints to being thorough in the early stages. Sequoia, which also undertakes governance training for founders and senior management, maintained that the company was, '…willing to do whatever it takes to encourage good behaviour.'[67]

This message can be interpreted as: there are two vectors to good governance—oversight governance and behavioural governance. What does behavioural corporate governance entail? It is a behavioural code—a set of guidelines—for what constitutes a good board and leadership behaviour before the rot of narcissism takes its toll. Multiple regulations improve oversight governance, but there is a lacuna in behavioural governance. Most boards are reluctant to interpret or act on significant behavioural aberrations. They wait for evidentiary proof.

The Sequoia blog may have awakened players in the corporate governance space and start-up ecosystem to address the subject with increasing urgency and seriousness. India's start-up ecosystem is at a nascent stage and is full of promise. Hence, it is essential

[65]'Corporate Governance: The Cornerstone of an Enduring Company', *YourStory*, 17 April 2022, https://tinyurl.com/5amf473t. Accessed on 8 July 2023.

[66]'Mike Moritz', *Charlie Rose*, https://tinyurl.com/s6wy9chr. Accessed on 8 July 2023.

[67]'Corporate Governance: The Cornerstone of an Enduring Company', *YourStory*, 17 April 2022, https://tinyurl.com/5amf473t. Accessed on 17 July 2023.

to minimize aberrations like Housing.com, BharatPe, Zilingo and Trell. These are a few Indian start-ups that failed due to fraud, mismanagement and poor governance. It is essential for board directors to act on any negative signals they pick up. (The directors' checklist provided in Chapter 3 to interpret early warning signals for corporates applies to start-ups too). Yet, doubtlessly, *ahankar-mukt* leadership that consciously keeps pride and ego at arm's length is essential although it may be difficult to achieve. Yet, how many leaders are able to implement such enlightened leadership?

Wisdom to Overcome Dysfunction

To improve credibility and governance, the wisdom underlying corporate regulations demands the presence of independent directors on the board. However, there has recently been increased disquiet about the inadequate role played by independent directors on boards. As an ancient sage is said to have noted, 'When honest people fail in their duty to speak up, they wound dharma and they ought to be punished.' Thus, there is an urgent need to bridge the gap between knowledge and action.

Every aspiring director should either be trained to be wise through an external source or should teach themselves the same. Corporations need 'wise' directors, but wisdom does not always equate to experience. Wisdom is action, which comes from belief not understanding. We can discover and activate wisdom within ourselves.[68]

One chooses to take the high road on the bedrock of humility, which encompasses the wisdom and ethics necessary to build trust and facilitate learning. Take the case of the Indian state after Partition. The Indian Constitution was framed around the

---

[68]Lickerman, Alex, 'Where Does Wisdom Come From?', *Psychology Today*, 20 October 2013, https://tinyurl.com/92pjw3sf. Accessed on 23 June 2023.

traditional concept of *vasudhaiva kutumbakam*. Our leaders did not, and still do not, want India to be a Hindu state although there was a concerted attempt to divide India and Pakistan along communal lines. Another example of humility in leadership is Jamsetji Tata stating, 'In a free enterprise, the community is not just another stakeholder, but is, in fact, the very purpose of its existence.'[69] Humility is evidently crucial for successful leadership. So, can it be developed?

Being Humble

If boards are about power and accomplishment, it would be naïve not to encounter narcissism and ego within them. No courses teach humility, except for the learnings of life. When Gopal confronted the impact of power during his days as CEO, he realized the dangers of arrogance. Consequently, he adopted a practice that, he hopes, positively promotes humility.

While visiting Casablanca on behalf of Tata Chemicals for a discussion about a joint venture, Gopal attended a dinner hosted by the chairman of the joint venture partner—a Moroccan mining company. As a sign of goodwill, the chairman gifted Gopal a frame made from animal remains—bones, teeth and nails—recovered in Morocco and carbon-dated to be 20 to 40 million years old. Some may consider this to be an odd gift. However, this 'unusual' artefact adorned Gopal's office till he retired because he considered it to be a legacy of the earth and the miracles of nature. Visitors would ask him, 'Why do you display this frame?' In response, Gopal would recount the history of the artefact and trace its origin back to the presence of the Mediterranean Sea in Morocco millions of years ago. Thus, for Gopal, the artefact was

---

[69]'Tata Steel's Sustainability Mission', *Tata Steel*, https://tinyurl.com/3hcdyfbt. Accessed on 8 July 2023.

a reminder of the frailty of humans before the infinite continuum of time, especially for leaders on the brink of what they may perceive as a momentous decision, which, in fact, is a mere cog in the wheel of time.

Another picture that inspires humility in Gopal is an image clicked by Carl Sagan: the 'Pale Blue Dot'. On 14 February 1990, as NASA's Voyager-1 was speeding away from earth, astronauts turned back to see the receding image of our home planet. It looked just like a pale blue dot in the vast emptiness of space. Later, Carl Sagan wrote, 'That's home. That's us. [...] The aggregate of our joy and suffering, thousands of confident religions, ideologies, and economic doctrines, every hunter and forager, every king and peasant[...]on a mote of dust suspended in a sunbeam. [...] The Earth is a very small stage in a vast cosmic arena.'[70]

If these perspectives do not demonstrate the insignificance of a person or dilute the narcissism of leaders, what else can? Humility can be learnt in the context of our purpose on this planet.

---

[70]'Carl Sagan: "The Earth Is a Very Small Stage in a Vast Cosmic Arena."', *FS*, https://tinyurl.com/2fbxyyb2. Accessed on 26 June 2023.

7

Signals: How to Read and
Deal with Them

In 2011, John Looker, a resident of Newark, Ohio, suffering from brain cancer, became a celebrity fundraiser to help fight cancer. He hosted charity events and raised millions of dollars from Americans. Some years later, though, a small club of doubters who respected patient privacy norms, wondered why Looker's cancer had not metastasized but sprung up every year just before a fundraising event. They started to question whether Looker even had cancer. Upon confrontation, Looker admitted to his lies. He had bluffed the cancer story and misused the funds. Thus, a bigger scam was averted.[71] Fortunately, such confrontation is usually the last resort, and there are more tactful ways to address signals of corporate malpractice.

---

[71]Ellin, Abby, 'He Was the Face of a Bike-a-thon to Fight Cancer. He was also a Fake.', *The New York Times*, 1 August 2019, https://tinyurl.com/2p8uf38w. Accessed on 5 July 2023.

The 5C Path to Action

It is crucial for directors on company boards to not ignore persistent and unusual behaviours. When they smell a rat, they must learn to rely on their intuition and respond responsibly to these signals. Watch carefully for the prodromal signals that usually portend an unusual development. So, how should directors translate their perception into action? How can they intervene?

We suggest a 5C action plan—consider, consult, counsel, coach and, if all fails, confront.

1. **Consideration** demands reading about the subject and scrutinizing its potential facets.
2. **Consultation** entails discussions with the management, experts or other directors to clarify any additional factors that may not have been considered by the individual director.
3. **Counselling** comes into play when there is an alternate point of view about which the director feels strongly.
4. **Coaching**, where required, involves the director training the CEO to see the 'other' perspective.
5. **Confronting** should only happen if the director detects rigidity or an alternate agenda. All the steps up to this point must be completed collaboratively and amicably.

Even if the evidence cannot be legally proved, directors should *act*. Boards are not ceremonial, they have obligations. Directors' actions must be based on facts and shared judgement—intuition based on facts that do not add up.

Almost every recent case of corporate governance failure had a trail of early signals that directors noticed leading up to the moment of crisis. The multinational financial services company, J.P. Morgan received an internal warning from its compliance officers about the risks of continuing to deal with their client

Jeffry Epstein, the billionaire financier and sex offender who died by suicide in a New York jail. However, no one within J.P. Morgan heeded these warnings. In fact, instead of exiting the relationship, senior executives at the company were blasé about Epstein's behaviour and would even joke about his interest in young girls.[72]

Similarly, consider the prodromal warnings in the cases of Ranbaxy, Jet Airways and YES Bank. It is usually after the disaster, when the media strings together the sequence of events, that it appears obvious for the board to have acted.

Toxic Leadership

Most directors are reluctant to not conform and start questioning the warning signals because they risk being the only dissenting voice in the room. This is true especially when they are dealing with a high performing CEO who may be arrogant, in-your-face, cocky and, above all, a shrewd strategist with control issues. At a governance conclave in Mumbai, participants debated on how to deal with a superlatively performing CEO who is arrogant. Let us look at the ongoing drama about a real institution, presented as if it were an imaginary company.

The CEO of this company consistently positioned it as the fastest growing corporation, particularly since he had taken over. Growth targets were announced with panache, accompanied by large-scale spending plans on grandiose projects. These were cheered on with great enthusiasm by credulous investors. The CEO oozed charisma and had a Demosthenes-like oratorial skill. He repeatedly pointed out that his predecessors were losers and

---

[72]Flitter, Emily, and Jessica Silver-Greenberg, 'JPMorgan Kept Jeffrey Epstein as a Client Despite Internal Warnings', *The New York Times*, 8 August 2019, https://tinyurl.com/5xmss5kn. Accessed on 8 July 2023.

kept promising to move fast and compensate for lost time. The CEO expressed his vision of quadrupling company value by 2030. Meanwhile, several prodromal signals had been emerging and accumulating.

1. While competitors faced business headwinds, the CEO did not even admit to a problem. This left his client-facing employees and business associates bewildered.

2. The CEO announced major projects involving significant overseas capital purchases. Unconfirmed and difficult-to-verify signals suggested that company procedures had been subverted for these acquisitions. The CEO, of course, strongly denied the allegations.

3. The chief accountant of the company observed that the deficit in the company cash flows was higher than what had been projected in the annual accounts. He felt that the barrier of prudent management had been breached by the real deficit. The CFO diplomatically responded that this would be 'investigated seriously'.

4. The company's former chief of business strategy later expressed doubts about the company's revenue recognition methodology. He believed that the growth needed to be corrected, as it had been overstated in the last few years.

5. The company had a risk management department, but its head and the deputy head had simmering differences of opinions and styles. These differences became public, causing directors to wonder whether this department was functioning reliably.

6. Some independent directors expressed concern about internal matters and the functioning of the board. The CEO soft-pedalled and agreed to investigate their complaints.

7. Another independent director, who chaired the board's treasury and risk management committee quit, and later

admitted to having serious differences with the CEO's perspective about prudent risk management.

8. In two independent communications, a group of suppliers and distributors expressed concern about the company's practices. As committed partners of the company, they wished to alert the management. This was strongly refuted by another group of suppliers and distributors, who expressed loyalty to the company, implying that the first group was disloyal.

Clearly, the directors of the organization ought to act on the 5C path.

In another such case, on 20 January 2019, *Los Angeles Times* carried a report about the allegedly toxic leadership style of an important public figure—the chancellor of the University of California—and its adverse impact on colleagues.[73] The chancellor demonstrated a dictatorial style and acted unilaterally, which was not acceptable in a research and educational institution, and caused discontent among colleagues. Neither the person nor the facts are personally known to us, but the report was an investigative response to the warning signs.

There is greater awareness today about toxic leaders and the possibility of autocratic CEOs who demonstrate a destructive leadership style, adversely impacting the company and shareholders. When this is sensed, boards can no longer turn a blind eye. They have to act in response, just as they would if they smelled something burning in their homes. Incidentally, the fire is may sometimes neither be scorching nor visible but is damaging all the same.

---

[73]Robbins, Gary, 'UC San Diego Chancellor Pradeep Khosla: Blunt-Spoken Visionary or Belittling Bully?', *Los Angeles Times*, 20 January 2019, https://tinyurl.com/4d556t4e. Accessed on 5 July 2023.

There's No Smoke Without Fire

A board member of a reputed trust recently asked Gopal, 'We hear about domination by our CEO, but he delivers results. We have learnt that if he is even slightly questioned, he becomes defensive and edgy, giving the impression of his way or the highway. As a board member what should I do?' This board member could sense the smoke but could not see any fires. In such a situation, what could he do?

The short answer is, if you smell smoke, continue sniffing around—be concerned, act and do not look helpless. The outside perception of a CEO being better than the internal perception is a prodromal signal. Experience has taught us that prodromal clues are always embedded in the leadership behaviour. There are four symptoms of a leader becoming toxic.

1. The leader enjoys a huge concentration of power. People in the organization are fearful of speaking up. Such a leader is often surrounded by a tale-bearing coterie. Think of the hush-hush behaviour among managers in some promoter-dominated companies. This is a worrying signal.

2. It is believed that the leader can do no wrong—they are deified. There is heavy image promotion by the corporate communications team. Think of Vijay Mallya, Rana Kapoor and the Singh brothers at Ranbaxy. Think also of the blusteringly ridiculous claims of Patanjali Ayurved and Baba Ramdev.

3. The leader constantly refers to a hidden threat, a 'competitive and devious force'. They attribute negative results to multiple factors, even acts of misfortune, but avoid taking responsibility themselves. Managers are expected to simply stop questioning and just close ranks against this unseen enemy.

4. There is visible degradation of the reputation and long-standing attributes of the organization. This could involve leverage on the balance sheet, excessive pledging of stocks, decline in product quality rankings, employee attrition and frequent departure of senior managers. There is a general air of hubris.

Beware of smooth-talking CEOs who name-drop, seek visibility and behave arrogantly. When the company does well, they imply that it is because of their vision and strategy. When the company runs into problems, they blame demonetization, Brexit, China, Ukraine—everything but themselves.

One of Gopal's friends who worked in the Navy mentioned that he judges the stability and balance of a ship by its wake—the symmetrical patterns on the surface of the water on which the ship has sailed. Some leaders leave a smooth and symmetrical wake behind them while others drench people and capsize other boats, disregarding the impact of their leadership size.

Gopal recollects his former boss who used to say, walk around a graveyard and you will find many who thought they were irreplaceable! In recent years, certain high-profile CEOs were lauded and feted as superlative, but the wake that they left behind is now visible to all. If the CEO leaves his people on choppy waters, directors must act. What can this action be?

An Action Plan for Directors

In his book titled *Exit, Voice and Loyalty*, Albert Hirschman, a political economist and intellectual, wrote about the two ways of reacting: quitting (exit) or speaking up (voice), both of which are influenced by loyalty. Institutional loyalty influences the manner of team members' exit—low loyalty results in a quiet exit, high loyalty leads to a visible exit. An unemotional relationship with the institution almost always leads to a quiet exit, which should always cause discomfort because it could be a sign of a brewing toxicity within the organization.

In December 2018, *mint* reported that 743 independent directors on Nifty-listed company boards had vacated their position before the end of their tenure, but 561 did so without adequate reasons.[74] However, the law requires independent directors to state a reason for quitting. The most common response to this was 'personal reasons and preoccupations'. The notable exceptions were a couple of directors of YES Bank and JM Financial Asset Reconstruction Company who stated they were stepping down due to inadequate governance. The crux of the matter is to rely on your inner voice. Act, talk, share or counsel, but please do not sit on the fence thinking. It is an uncomfortable position to find yourself in, but it is necessary to act for public good and to ease your conscience.

Former White House Counsel John Dean had testified before the US Congress in 1973 against the criminal conduct of the sitting President Richard Nixon, which eventually led to Nixon's exit. In 2019, Dean wrote an opinion piece in *The New York Times* to advise the contemporary White House Counsel Michael Cohen, who similarly testified before the Congress about the then sitting President Donald Trump. He stated, '...if Mr. Trump is removed from office, or defeated in 2020, in part because of his testimony, he [Cohen] will be reminded of it for the rest of his life. [...] he will always live in this pigeonhole. How do I know this? I am still dealing with it.'[75] It does seem that right actions are important, even if they are uncomfortable and loaded with consequences.

---

[74]Upadhyay, Jayshree P., 'Why Independent Directors Are Rushing for the Exit Door', *mint*, 18 December 2018, https://tinyurl.com/2f29pssw. Accessed on 8 July 2023.
[75]Dean, John W., 'John Dean: I Testified Against Nixon. Here's My Advice for Michael Cohen.', *The New York Times*, 1 March 2019, https://tinyurl.com/yee52jsh. Accessed on 8 July 2023.

The Distant Rumbling of Thunder

Every crisis that appears unique to a current leader, has occurred in the past. There is very little about the human experience that has not happened before. The conviction that the present problem is unique and unprecedented is what makes it difficult for people to share their fears. Just like the distant rumblings of thunder, which warn of possible rain long before a torrential deluge, warning signs may appear weak initially but need to be acknowledged. For instance, when even a veiled criticism of a much-admired leader results in prompt rejection of the alternate view.

Another great example of the need to heed warning signs comes from Satyajit Ray's *Ashani Sanket,* which means signals of thunder or distant thunder, based on Bibhutibhushan Bandopadhyay's short-story. It tells the story of the man-made Bengal famine of 1943 in which 5 million people died of starvation. Set in the 1940s, the film depicts life in a small village during the Second World War, when the colonial government hoarded the civilian food supply for its armies. The protagonists of the film, a Brahmin and his wife, have been leading an idyllic life in a village, where they are respected for their service to the community. The first sign of the impending crisis is a visitor devouring a simple meal while reporting that his village, neighbouring theirs, has been facing a shortage of rice. Soon after, the news of the food shortage spreads like wildfire and panic sets in. Traders start hiding their stocks for profits and the organized life of the village undergoes unexpected turmoil.

An added layer of complexity arises from the fact that people tend to develop different perceptions based on the same facts. Consider the examples listed below.

1. When the German Parliament likened the current Ukraine food grains situation to the 1930s famine in Ukraine,

caused by Josef Stalin's policies, Russia rejected the point of view.

2. When nationalist Indians blamed Sir Winston Churchill for diverting Bengal's food supplies to Britain's efforts in the Second World War, the colonial power rejected any criticism of their war hero.

3. During the late 1880s, when Dadabhai Naoroji propounded his 'drain theory', arguing that Britain was steadily draining India's resources, he was ignored and pooh-poohed by the British establishment.

4. When an Israeli film juror offered his view on the aesthetics and motivations of the Indian film, *The Kashmir Files*, his view was rejected and criticized.

5. A film titled *Farha*, exposing Israel's treatment and killings of Palestinian refugees, was strongly protested in Israel.

Not Hardwired for Criticism

In the context of the warning sign, no viewpoint can be completely objective. It will always be interpreted subjectively and only time can bear testimony to how the perception turns out. Take the case of Jack Welch, the remarkable chairman and CEO of GE, who enjoyed a 20-year-long tenure from 1981 to 2001, during which he transformed GE into a fast-growing company in a slow-growth economy. Welch is credited to have grown GE's market capitalization to over $450 billion, of which about 40 per cent was in financial services (making money out of money). During his chairmanship, an analyst asked him whether the reliance on financial services was sustainable for GE and what he would do if, after his tenure, his successor reassessed the importance of GE's financial services business differently? Welch's response seemed to imply that if a successor did that, it would reflect poorly on his own choice of successor.[76] Now we all know that GE's decline accelerated during the 2008 recession while losses by the GE Capital financial segment nearly sank the company. By 2015, Jeff Immelt, Welch's successor was forced to judge that the financial services side of the business was indeed unsustainable.

It is apparent that those in power generally do not engage with critics with appropriate urgency. It is because they mistake warnings as dissent or political opposition designed to stall their progress. They believe they are on the fast track and are afraid to slow down, not realizing that constructive criticism can be instrumental in changing bad practices.

Our minds are trained to reject a diversity of views or criticism due to social inputs, including prioritizing quick results. To counteract this, we need to develop a scientific bend of mind. One of Gopal's former senior colleagues, who was a scientist, defined a scientific bend of mind as such: 'One should have large sympathies for a diversity of beliefs without reserving the largest for one's own.' This applies to practitioners of corporate governance as well.

Leaders need to interact with alternative ideas and idea-makers, which, in turn, helps generate ideas for action. While leaders should be more receptive of criticism, directors should not hesitate to act on any warning signals and should voice their concerns rather than wait for a crisis to disrupt the status quo.

The Moral Response

When Gopal used to visit Bulgaria in the 1980s, he would often hear an expression about bears that loosely translated to: 'when the bear dances in your neighbour's garden, it will soon be dancing in yours for sure'. This saying applies to the corporate world as well.

---

[76]Dubner, Stephen J., 'Extra: Jack Welch Full Interview', *Freakonomics*, 18 Match 2018, https://tinyurl.com/5246exrb. Accessed on 8 July 2023.

Public reports of disputes and business surprises distract company managements. They also dilute the confidence of investors, lenders and the ecosystem. Remember what happened with Infosys when its directors were sparring between 2016 and 2017? The actions and decisions of the board did not find favour with the original shareholders of Infosys and compelled the CEO, Vishal Sikka, to resign. Similarly, Ranbaxy's global head Dinesh Thakur blew the whistle on dubious manufacturing practices and fudged data provided to the Food and Drug Administration (FDA). Such reports certainly do not augur well for the company, in which case what should an independent director do? The developments may appear to be legal, but what if the consequences stretch minority shareholders' interests to the limit? The independent directors must look for patterns because there is always a pattern to such events. Given below is a hypothetical (not entirely) example.

Imagine a listed company where there are two promoter-shareholders, A and B—a bit like Indigo Airlines. The retail shareholders can be aggregated together as C. Assume that A, B and C each have one-third share in the company. The law requires all directors to act in the company's overall interest, but within this obligation, A and B are likely to act in their favour. C are required to act in the interest of the minority shareholders and must judge signals on this basis.

C notices growing and disturbing signals of directors A and B developing a difference of opinion, strong enough for them to litigate without directly involving the company board. What, then, is the duty of the independent directors to protect minority shareholders' interests? It could well appear that the dispute is outside the company and the independent directors have little or no role. This is not true. Independent directors should avoid taking sides in the dispute, as they would with a neighbour couple who have unresolvable quarrels. However, using common sense, independent directors can consider a three-step action plan.

1. **Persuasion:** Independent directors, collectively or individually, could try to persuade the directors representing the disputants to step off the board while they sort out their differences through dialogue, arbitration or litigation. This may help sequestrate the company from media reports. A and B could return to the board after sorting out differences. C has no legal right to seek this action or to enforce it, but they can make a request, although it may be ignored or rejected.

2. **Apprehension:** As a next step, independent directors could write to regulatory or empowered agencies with their apprehension about a decline in share prices. As directors A and B are on the board, maybe the agency like to intervene. The regulator or agency too may ignore or reject this request.

3. **Resignation:** As a final step, the independent directors, collectively or individually, could resign from the board. They should not quote the lame duck excuse that they have other priorities. Rather, they should transparently state their apprehension as the law demands. This can serve as the caveat emptor for retail investors. A and B would surely not appreciate this intervention but may feel pressured to resolve the differences and avert an adverse outcome.

Borrowing from Professor Eugene Soltes' book[77], silent independent directors might regard a sticky situation as a business problem and distance themselves; but even inaction could constitute a moral failing. In the case of ICICI Bank's loan scam, involving non-disclosures by the board and Jet Airways' bankruptcy, the actions taken to uphold minority shareholders' rights were not clear. On the other hand, independent directors

---

[77] Soltes, Eugene, *Why They Do It: Inside the Mind of the White-Collar Criminal*, PublicAffairs, 2016.

at CG Power and Industrial Solutions noted the financial irregularities and responded by removing the chairman. If independent directors adopt an appropriate and calibrated approach, they can develop a moral response as the ominous signals develop. Think of IL&FS, YES Bank or even the fraud at Punjab and Maharashtra Co-operative (PMC) Bank that created fictitious accounts to hide loans worth over ₹4,000 crore extended to its nearly bankrupt parent company, Housing Development and Infrastructure Limited (HDIL).[78] In each of these cases, the warning signals were apparent well before matters spun out of control and came crashing into the public domain.

Sometimes, the government makes profits by selling its PSU shares to another PSU, which it then reports as revenue in its budget accounts. Recall LIC buying IDBI (Industrial Development Bank of India) shares or BPCL (Bharat Petroleum Corporation Limited) shares being bought by ONGC (Oil and Natural Gas Corporation)? While practices like these may be permissible, they are morally questionable. What moral authority does the government have to reprimand companies for doing such things? Thus, moral rectitude is equally essential for the government.

Listen to the Kibitzers

Kibitzer is a Yiddish word for a spectator of bridge or chess who offers unsolicited advice during the game. It can also be applied to businesses. Some leaders respond positively to unsolicited comments from such kibitzers. They consider them to be signals from the ground and incorporate the message into their transformation programme. Following is a list of examples of

---

[78]Shah, Charul, 'PMC Bank Fraud: "Officials Knew of Hidden HDIL Loan Accounts Since 2017"', *Hindustan Times*, 28 December 2019, https://tinyurl.com/bdf5st6s. Accessed on 17 July 2023.

major corporate transformation or crisis management done based on inputs from such kibitzers.

1. J.J. Irani, known as the Steel Man of India, reinvented Tata Steel in the 2000s.
2. Larsen & Toubro CEO S.N. Subramanyan acquired Mindtree in 2019.
3. Billionaire activist–investor Nelson Peltz of Trian Fund Management, who acquired a majority stake in PepsiCo, pushed hard for the company to split its food and beverages division in 2013. Indra Nooyi, then PepsiCo CEO, engaged in this tussle and conducted an exhaustive strategic review but did not give in to the risky proposal, thereby compelling Peltz to sell his shares and leave.
4. Ellen Kullman, chairman of Dupont, an American conglomerate, successfully repelled Peltz's attempt to join their board.
5. Unilever engaged and fended off the bid by Brazilian investor 3G and Kraft Heinz. 3G had bought Kraft, engineered its merger with Heinz and run the company to the ground.
6. Klaus Kleinfeld, CEO of Alcoa, an American aluminium company, got trapped in his dealings with Elliot Management, a financial company that had invested in Alcoa. Kleinfeld had to step down from his position when he expressed his belief that Elliot Management had been snooping into his personal matters involving his young daughter, which was difficult to prove.
7. Tom Buckner at AkzoNobel, the Dutch paint manufacturer, responded to the bid by an American paints major by divesting Akzo's valuable chemicals business on being pressurized by investors who were critical of the company's economic performance.

The importance of listening to kibitzers can be demonstrated by another story about the subsonic listening of pigeons, and what happens when it fails. The World Pigeon Racing competition had been effectively going on for over a century. However, during the 1997 race from France to England, across the English Channel, most pigeons failed to reach England—an unprecedented disaster. It appeared that the pigeons' navigation system could not discern familiar subsonic signals from the ocean waves crashing into the coast. This was because a supersonic Concorde had left Heathrow around 11.00 a.m. and emitted its own subsonic signals as it broke the sound barrier. Thus, the pigeons, seemingly confused by the plane's subsonic signals, had lost their way.

Likewise, in companies, a CEO receives subsonic sounds from the kibitzers, including employees, customers and business observers. Good CEOs realize that nobody is too small to make an impact. Investors and analysts have the power to greatly pressure the board through their comments and demands. Boards cannot be dismissive and must respond astutely.

Since the kibitzer model is effective, how does one ensure that there is no dearth of them in an organization? The case study method has been widely and successfully used in management education, and one of its unintended effects is it helps people become critical commentators or kibitzers. Gopal recalls his training days when he found fault with various CEOs while discussing their case studies. He states: 'Heaven knows how stupid I must have appeared to my team while they observed my decision-making and actions as a CEO!'

CEO Narcissism

Offering critiques in newspapers, writing case studies and doing television commentaries—all kibitzer activities—are a lot easier than actually doing the job. Yet, however annoying their suggestions may be, kibitzers should not be ignored. A controlled degree of narcissism is essential for a CEO to be successful. However, a CEO's deafness to kibitzer signals comes from the natural narcissism that accompanies power. Controlling this narcissism is a good start to openly hearing subsonic signals.

CEO narcissism manifests based on seven skills: ruthlessness, charm, focus, mental toughness, fearlessness, action and mindfulness. Most leaders are familiar with all seven skills through their experiences as a CEO. Professional psychiatrists are of the view that narcissists and psychopaths have similar personality traits. Both have a high self-opinion along with a low opinion of others. They always credit success to themselves while failures are always attributed to external factors. Within a limit, these characteristics work positively. However, if that boundary is breached, the same characteristics can be damaging.

The Perils of an 'Indispensable' CEO

Leadership is glamorous and CEO is an aspirational title. There is a halo around leaders and CEOs. However, they also risk disrepute, whether fair or unfair, during their tenure or even long after (think of GE's Jack Welch). He was infamous for his explosive temper. He argued his way from one decision to the next, terrorized subordinates and even made his allies cower in fear. As one GE employee said during his heydays: 'Jack comes on like a herd of elephants.'[79]

Certainly, there are risks to being CEO. It's an impossible job, as every day is a trial by fire. One must make quick decisions, deliver positive results, face enormous pressures and, worst of all, strike a balance between the board and management. CEOs

---

[79]Gelles, David, 'What Jack Welch Got Wrong (Just About Everything)', *LinkedIn*, 31 May 2022, https://tinyurl.com/2xxrwabj. Accessed on 8 July 2023.

can rarely make everyone happy and, thus, they are always at risk of being removed.

According to a CNBC report, in 2019, 1,600 CEOs left their jobs, voluntarily or involuntarily.[80] One of the most damaging exits was one in which an iconic CEO, presented as irreplaceable by the media or sycophants, was removed from this position. Parting with a CEO is mostly hard on the company, but especially so when a CEO is forced to leave because a board made the wrong choice. Hopefully, directors possess the humility to accept their error, though such humility is rarely visible. If there is an ethical transgression, it is easy to deal with, but if there is a performance or behavioural transgression the options can get complicated.

We have witnessed the dilemma of parting with a CEO several times. In one case, the CEO's integrity was being doubted. After extensive discussions, the directors unanimously concluded to act. Sensitive execution avoided corporate reputational consequences, yet signalled to specific ethics to the employees.

Another such case involved the CEO's performance and behaviour. To discuss this matter, the directors needed to trust each other. However, the recently appointed directors did not vote because it protected their personal credibility. Regardless, the tenured directors participated in the discussions. Counselling, coaching and notice followed sequentially. At the crucial board meeting, the tenured directors' votes were unanimous. The decision was implemented with no reputational consequences. A crude test of the validity of this decision was that managers from the company were not surprised by the board's action. The message was clear—performance and behaviour matter. This board spent

---

[80]Fitzgerald, Maggie, '2019 Had the Most CEO Departures on Record with More than 1,600', *CNBC*, 7 January 2020, https://tinyurl.com/ycs6u7zx. Accessed on 8 July 2023.

as much time on making the decision as on elegantly executing it. The directors were sensitive to the devastation employees would experience due to a shocking change. The key lessons were based on open discussions, executed with grace and minimized negatives for employees.

It is distressingly frequent for the root cause of a CEO exit to be a personality conflict. For instance, Chris Viehbacher shifted to Sanofi from GSK with the brief to make the culture less French. According to reports, he parted because he was 'insufficiently French'! Thierry Bolloré, former CEO of the Renault Group, left because his board felt he had been an acolyte of the arrested former chairman, Carlos Ghosn. A few months after Citigroup acquired Vikram Pandit's hedge fund, he was invited to become CEO of the organization. However, a new chairman, Michael O'Neill, manoeuvred to remove Pandit because he was irked by Pandit's divestment plans to solve the organization's problems.[81]

On a lighter note, do you know what Viehbacher, Bolloré, Pandit and a lot of other foreign CEOs have in common? October is a particularly inauspicious month for them all. All of the following CEOs have quit their jobs in October: Jacques Nasser from Ford (2000), Michael Ovitz from Disney (1996), Adam Neumann from WeWork (2019) and Mike Parker from Nike (2019). So, CEOs, beware the ides of October!

Firing is acceptable, but only as a last resort.[82] Nothing is worse than a clumsily executed good decision. While a board has the legal right to ask a CEO to leave, it has the moral duty to do it the right way—neeyat matters, so does neeti. A righteous decision aligned with the right way should be the mantra. The social mores,

---

[81]Gopalakrishnan, R., *Crash: Lessons from the Entry and Exit of CEOs*, Penguin Random House India, 2018.

[82]'Leadership Lapses: When Is Firing the Right Response?', *Knowledge at Wharton*, 12 September 2017, https://tinyurl.com/3hzxhvsj. Accessed on 8 July 2023.

the organization's culture and values and the ethical principles are significant during decision-making and implementation.

Myrmidons of the CEO

A myrmidon is someone who is unquestioning and subservient towards a powerful leader. Rooted in Greek mythology, myrmidons are known for their loyalty to their leaders. They fought under Achilles's leadership during the Trojan War. Achilles, the son of the Greek King Poleus, was immortal. This was because his mother, the sea nymph Thetis, dipped him in sacred waters while holding him by his heel. Thus, his body, barring his heel, became invulnerable. This is where the phrase 'Achilles heel', meaning an inherent weakness in an individual, comes from. Similarly, myrmidons can also become a leader's weakness.

Reflect on powerful people like CEOs, ministers, bureaucrats, academics, actors and sportspeople. Too many leaders are visibly trapped amid a swarm of myrmidons, a bit like bees on a honeycomb. They often irrationally boost CEOs egos. Such CEOs must be protected from myrmidons.

In 1991, Unilever launched the detergent Persil Power in the UK against P&G's Ariel Ultra, a formidable competitor. Persil Power contained a manganese-based catalyst that helped unleash its bleaching power. Regrettably, when it was used, clothes first lost their colour and then their structural integrity as the formulation was too strong. In an unusual move, the chairman of P&G Edward Arzt flew to London to draw Unilever's attention to their inadvertently dangerous formulation. Misreading the situation, Unilever's myrmidons gleefully rejoiced that their product had made the FMCG giant P&G nervous. They advised the chairman of Unilever Michael Perry to ignore P&G and disregard their nervous warning. However, after four disastrous years of selling the flawed product, Perry magnanimously admitted at an annual general meeting that Persil Power was 'one of the greatest marketing setbacks Unilever had experienced'.

History is littered with examples of those who refused to be mere myrmidons. For instance, the story of Archbishop St Thomas of Canterbury (1119–1170) from medieval England. King Henry II, to increase his control over the Christian Church, appointed the priest Thomas Becket as the Archbishop of Canterbury, expecting the latter to be a myrmidon. But Becket chose to place the Church and conscience above submission to royalty. At the Constitution of Clarendon, Becket declined to comply when officials asked him to agree to the King's right to curb the power of the Church. When informed about the Archbishop's refusal, the frustrated King despairingly said, 'Will no one rid me of this turbulent priest?' Four zealous knights, who overheard the anguished king, being myrmidons in their own right, stealthily killed the Archbishop in the cathedral.

Before electing a director, particularly an independent one, to a company's board, it is important to diligently assess their potential to turn into myrmidons. This can be assessed based on several factors, including the directors' culture and belief systems. For instance, shareholders in India cannot expect high levels of candour and outspokenness from directors because, even though Indian historical texts prescribe the path of truth, they also underline being gentle with others. The dharma of Hindus is very clearly described in the Manu Smriti (4.138, verse 4), as: 'Speak the truth in a way that is pleasing to others. Do not speak the truth in a manner that is injurious. Never speak untruth, though it may be expressed pleasantly. This is the eternal path of morality and dharma.'[83] A similar sentiment is expressed in the Bhagavad Gita (17–15), where Lord Krishna advises, 'Express

---

[83]Jha, Ganganatha, *Manusmriti with the Commentary of Medhatithi*, University of Calcutta, 1920.

yourself in words that do not cause distress, and which are truthful, inoffensive and beneficial.'[84]

While these quotes indicate that Indians are culturally conditioned to be gentle in the way they communicate dissent, it does not mean that they are prone to being myrmidons. In fact, these quotes emphasize the importance of the rare skill of disagreeing without becoming disagreeable. Thus, growing up in such a cultural background and being conditioned to believe in the qualities of gentleness, Indian directors are likely to speak truth to power but gently and diplomatically.

Knowing the risk myrmidons pose to any business, what can wise leaders do to rectify their influence? First, they can recognize that they are an inevitable accessory of power and that their power invisibly affects even the wisest leader. Next, here are some tangible steps you can take to minimize their ill-effects:

1. encourage listening skills by allowing and fostering alternative views;
2. separate the roles of the chairman and CEO to make discussions more open and transparent; and
3. ensure gender-based and professional diversity in skills, talent and knowledge.

Separation of the Board and the Management

The board and management play different roles in the efficient functioning of a corporation, which must be respected. An excellent allegory for this point can be found in the UK's governance model. In their governance system, the prime minister symbolizes efficiency and is answerable to the people, while the monarch imparts dignity to that efficiency and is answerable to God. Applying this idea

---

[84]'Chapter 17: Śhraddhā Traya Vibhāg Yog', *Bhagavad Gita*, https://tinyurl.com/2hpje87u. Accessed on 17 July 2023.

into the realm of corporate governance, the CEO should represent efficiency and report to the board while the board should dignify the efficiency and be answerable to the shareholders.

Statutory obligations should be discharged wisely by CEOs and boards. When the tension between opposing views is all pervading, a valid test for any decision is whether it balances efficiency and dignity. To illustrate this point, let us look at the stint of one of the most infamous HP CEOs.

In 1999, Carly Fiorina was lured from her senior position at AT&T to join HP as its CEO. Her brief was to be a 'real change agent' for the company. Fiorina took the mandate seriously. Within a slow work culture, she rapidly identified and executed many improvements and corrective steps related to organization and processes. Management analysis and initiatives suggested the possibility of a beneficial merger with Compaq, the second biggest PC manufacturer at the time. She became convinced that the merger would be, 'a decisive move that accelerates our strategy and positions us to win by offering even greater value to our customers and partners'.[85] The board unanimously voted in favour of the HP–Compaq merger. This was confirmed by the executive vice president (EVP) and Director of HP Richard Hackborn, who said, 'The board thoroughly analysed the transaction and unanimously concluded that this is the best way to deliver value that our shareholders expect.'[86]

However, after the decision was announced, it was opposed from various quarters. Some statements suggested that although the decision of the board had formally been unanimous, several directors privately had reservations about it. Hackborn recalled

---

[85]'H-P, Compaq Agree to $25 Billion Merger', *CNN*, 4 September 2001, https://tinyurl.com/3f65a8fs. Accessed on 8 July 2023.

[86]Gopalakrishnan, R., 'Balancing Act', *Business Standard*, 6 July 2018, https://tinyurl.com/3wjk5v39. Accessed on 8 July 2023.

that he had also been unsure of the success of the merger, 'We all had reservations. None of us was convinced that Compaq was the exact right answer at the start.'[87] Independent Director Robert Knowling said that, initially, he had been neutral to the idea. However, over time, he was convinced that the merger would improve HP's competitive positioning. Another independent Director, Philip Conduit, stated that the proposal was not without risk but that the opportunity outweighed the risk.

The family trusts of the founders (Hewlett and Packard), which held 15 per cent of the shares, opposed the deal. David Packard Jr stated, 'For some time I have been sceptical about management's confidence that it can aggressively reinvent HP culture overnight.'[88] Bill Hewlett critiqued, 'Compaq is a PC company and not very profitable.'[89] He also opined that the merger would be a distraction due to cultural clashes. The markets, too, gave the merger a thumbs down, evidenced by the drop in HP stock value by 30 per cent in a short time after the merger was announced. Dell chief, Michael Dell, called it 'the dumbest deal of the decade.'[90] Despite the criticism, Fiorina continued to lobby in favour of the deal. Finally, the directors voted, and the decision was carried by a narrow, Brexit-like margin of 51:49.

The post-merger years were a troubled period for HP because the financial results of the merger were way below expectation. This was worsened by the uncertainties of the business environment post-9/11. Disappointed by the results, Fiorina was pressured to

---

[87]Lohr, Steve, 'It's the Scion vs. the Board in Merger Fight', *The New York Times*, 4 February 2002, https://tinyurl.com/ydwnrc9x. Accessed on 8 July 2023.

[88]'Sons Blast Computer Merger', *CBS News*, 7 November 2001, https://tinyurl.com/ye22pvn7. Accessed on 8 July 2023.

[89]Gopalakrishnan, R., 'Balancing Act', *Business Standard*, 6 July 2018, https://tinyurl.com/3wjk5v39. Accessed on 8 July 2023.

[90]Rogers, James, 'Dell CEO Disses HP... Again', *The Street*, 19 August 2011, https://tinyurl.com/3bmx5mva. Accessed on 8 July 2023.

resign by the directors who had mandated her 'to transform HP' and change its culture. Fiorina left HP with a severance package in 2005.

However, three years after Fiorina's exit, the merger was declared to be very successful. *Huffington Post* carried the headline, 'Merger That Worked: Compaq and Hewlett Packard'.[91] As they say in India, '*Samay bada balwaan* (Time is a powerful judge)'. By the time Mark Hurd was HP's CEO, analysts commented, 'Carly made the merger happen despite fierce opposition. However, she lacked the skills to make the merger successful.'[92] Whether the independent directors at HP behaved wisely is up for judgement.

The Revered or Reverent CEO

CEOs can evoke the reverence of their boards of directors for several reasons. One of them could be if a CEO practises a different set of 5Cs—competence, clan, connections, charisma or a combination of them all.

It is challenging for any board to deal with a revered CEO. Especially, if the CEO is God-like and under the spell of another godman. Think of how the Aztecs lost Mexico under the spell of their deity Huitzilopochtli or the way Czar Nicholas lost Russia under the spell of the mystic Rasputin, who befriended the royal family and led them to their downfall.

How do you recognize when a powerful leader comes under the manipulative influence of another person? The situation could be tricky. Two such cases that reached the courts illustrate the undue influence of such factors on the corporate leader.

---

[91] Rosen, Ben, 'The Merger That Worked: Compaq and Hewlett-Packard', *HuffPost*, 19 August 2011, https://tinyurl.com/4se28wr8. Accessed on 8 July 2023.

[92] Gopalakrishnan, R., *Crash: Lessons from the Entry and Exit of CEOs*, Penguin Random House India, 2018.

Some years ago, a controversy broke out about Priyamvada Birla's estate and her chartered accountant turned confidante, Rajendra Singh Lodha.[93] Lodha had served as a non-executive director of the Birla Corporation. Lodha was very close to Priyamvada Birla and M.P. Birla, who were childless. He referred to her as Badi Ma. After M.P. Birla's death, Priyamvada Birla became the group chairman. At her initiative, the board appointed Lodha as co-chairperson of Birla Corporation. On her death, she left her estate of 5,000 crores to be handled by Lodha, an outsider to the Birla family. The family believed that Lodha had exercised a not-so-benign influence on the group chairperson after the death of her husband. Today, Rajendra Lodha's son, Harsh Lodha has inherited the claim to the Birla Corporation from his father. Commentators and observers have wondered what the board of directors had been doing when the company management was handed over to Lodha.

In another such example, the billionaire Singh brothers, Malvinder and Shivinder, reportedly squandered $2 billion of company wealth, partly through bad loans to the godman–business tycoon Baba Gurinder Singh Dhillon.[94] Dhillon, in addition to being related to one of the Singh brothers, reportedly deeply influenced and was involved in the financial affairs of the Singh brothers. One cannot help but wonder: what were the independent directors doing while loans from listed companies were being given without due diligence to a godman? Possibly, these reverent leaders were too powerful to be questioned or too magnetic for any director to come in their way.

---

[93]Dutt, Ishita Ayan, '40 years ago... and Now: Birlas—A Family that Hit the Headlines over a Will', *Rediff.com*, 26 November 2014, https://tinyurl.com/5essn2es. Accessed on 5 July 2023.

[94]Altstedter, Ari, 'The Billionaires and the Guru: How a Family Burned through $2 Billion', *Bloomberg*, 16 August 2018, https://tinyurl.com/yckdzh36. Accessed on 16 July 2023.

Similarly, France was shaken by an allegation about the L'Oréal heiress, Liliane Bettencourt coming under the influence of a gay society photographer François-Marie Banier. Subsequently, her daughter argued in court that her mother was no longer fit to manage the family fortune.

In all these cases, an important leader was being manipulated. As the malevolent influence on a leader develops, the facts are often not clear to independent directors and they may hesitate to discuss or do something. However, when a director suspects undue influence being exerted on the leader, they must act. In doing so, time is of the essence. If directors intervene too early, they can be accused of interfering with the personal affairs of the leader without evidence, which is a strong enough accusation for it to be escalated to the courts. If they do not intervene at all, independent directors can be criticized for sleeping at the wheel.

Warning Signs of Undue Influence

Unexpected outcomes may be expected when a leader is manipulated. People around the leader feel uneasy but find it difficult to understand the facts, and figure out a way to address the problem. How can a company's independent directors think about the issue if they don't understand signals of a powerful leader being under the negative influence of another person. Considering historical narratives, the early signals and order of such undue influence developing are likely to be:

1. Events compelling a powerful leader to face a huge personal chasm or void in his or her life.
2. A simple, humble and sometimes occult person enters the leader's life to fill that void.
3. This person starts gaining immense credibility and gravitas because the leader visibly treats them better than everyone else, for no apparent reason.

4. This person starts deploying their newfound surrogate power to the great consternation and annoyance of the others in the institution.

5. When the powerful leader dies or is removed, this person is dealt with and often consigned to history.

When an independent director perceives that a powerful leader of the board is being manipulated by another, they should cross-check the level of influence with the signals listed above. It is important that directors remain alert about behavioural changes in a powerful leader—a situation that could require quiet intervention and sagacity.

Hang the CEO

The Economist carried a business story titled 'Horrible Bosses' on board actions about CEOs' behaviours.[95] Are bosses becoming more unethical or insensitive than before? The authors' instinct tells us 'no', that is not so. The hard truth is that the transgressions of yesterday are no longer accepted today. CEOs need to understand this reality. If a Harold Geneen (ITT Corporation) or Jack Welch (GE), both harsh, plain-speaking CEOs were to operate in the same position today, and in the same way as they reportedly did decades ago, their behaviour and style would likely be unacceptable. Bosses are being held more accountable by the board for their behaviour and language with colleagues. Directors, too, want to encourage a healthy company environment to avoid getting sued and to protect the corporate brand, which has been built over a long time.

Harmful behaviours by CEOs attract huge media attention and the negative effect on company reputation festers for long.

---

[95]'Horrible Bosses', *The Economist*, 17 October 2012, https://tinyurl.com/4se28wr8. Accessed on 8 July 2023.

Before allowing any dust to be kicked up in the public domain, boards and CEOs must consider the severe damage to corporate brand and image. CEOs are hung in the court of public opinion long before the courts of law can pass judgment. Boards feel pressured to act soon and, in a manner that not only meets legal requirements but also has public approval. It is a tough act. A response like, 'Leave it to the board. We have investigated, nothing is wrong but regret that further details cannot be revealed,' no longer passes muster.

Unlike our defence forces, which have inherited extended colonial processes of formal and transparent procedures for enquiry, escalation and court martial, the response to allegations of problematic behaviours in corporations are flexible. Companies need a formalized internal code of behaviour and to better enforce the code. Regrettably, the latter is lacking even in some big companies. The code must be based on cultural factors, in addition to laws.

8

Succession: A Legacy of
Leadership

A family fights for control of its company amid uncertainty about the health of its patriarch. This is the theme of the HBO television show *Succession*, inspired by the stories of succession at two media conglomerates—the Murdochs' Twenty-First Century Fox and Sumner Redstone's Viacom. Reflecting real corporate life, the message of the show is clear: succession planning is essential but always tricky to implement. It cannot be too soon, yet one cannot rush into it. It also helps when the current leader supports the successor. As two academics, James Champy and Nitin Nohria, wrote, 'To feel threatened by one's successor is a futile but remarkably common reaction to inevitable departure.'[96] As board nomination committees across the world grapple with choosing the next leader, it is a booming time for tales of corporate succession. Experience, however, recommends a holistic agenda not only for succession but also for the predecessor's exit planning.

---

[96]Champy, James, and Nitin Nohria, *The Arc Of Ambition: Defining The Paths to Achievement: Defining the Leadership Journey*, Basic Books, 2000.

Regulators, accountants and lawyers occupy the field of corporate governance. The real practitioners of governance—board directors and operational leaders—should also get to express views from their perspective. Their wisdom comes from their practice, which could provide useful lessons in succession planning. We've discussed some key points to keep in mind during succession planning.

Clean Exits Ease Succession Pangs

Good, clean succession requires the choice of a successor to be clear along with the predecessor departing gracefully. If either falter, the process may collapse. Sycophants may easily persuade successful leaders that competent successors are unavailable when the truth may be that the leader has made it so. In our experience, in almost all cases, the non-availability of a successor is the predecessor's failure.

It is rare for both the predecessor and the successor to continue a legacy of success, although there are some unique exceptions. For instance, the iconic Walt Disney Company was being led by Chairman Michael Eisner since 1984. When Eisner retired in 2005, his successor, Bob Iger, successfully steered Disney to continue being a hugely valuable and successful company. However, Iger fumbled when it came to selecting and supporting his own successor.

On the other hand, in May 2018, CNBC carried an online story on the success of Unilever's CEO Paul Polman. He inherited 'a moribund company with declining revenues' in January 2009, and turned it around into a 'powerhouse'. The piece went on to add, 'Unilever has risen above the pack [...] everything traces to the leadership of Paul Polman for the past decade'.[97] Doubtlessly,

---

[97]George, Bill, 'As Consumer Giants Struggle, Unilever Rises Above the Pack', *CNBC*, 25 May 2018, https://tinyurl.com/78srbcwn. Accessed on 10 July 2023.

Polman had a vision and execution plan but he also enjoyed the freedom to execute under the superintendence of the board. It takes many years—nine, in this case—to judge the success of succession. Former Unilever Chairman Mike Angus used to say that the success of a CEO candidate is visible only when the chosen CEO's successor is regarded as successful. Tested against this lofty standard that judges success through three successive CEOs, most successions show cracks.

At Hindustan Unilever (HUL), Prakash Tandon took over the top job in 1961. He was followed by Vasant Rajadhyaksha, T. Thomas, Ashok Ganguly, Susim Datta and others. The distinctive aspect about each transition has been that the succession has involved a clean exit of the predecessor from the affairs of the company, which many find difficult to handle.

To understand this better, let us look at Louis Begley's novel *About Schmidt,* which was adapted into an Academy Award-winning film in 2002, starring Jack Nicholson. The film's protagonist, Warren Schmidt, retires from his managerial position in a life insurance company but finds it difficult to adjust to life thereafter. He periodically visits his young successor to offer advice and help, but his overtures are politely declined. Seeking meaning in life, he sponsors a Tanzanian child. He also disapproves of his daughter's choice of life partner. Despite his professional accomplishments, Schmidt begins to wonder whether he will be remembered for having made a difference to anyone. Aren't there too many Warren Schmidts among us, who find it difficult to take a clean break from work? It is the same with exiting CEOs.

Teacher, ex-Marine and author David Heenan, stated that most leaders could be characterized into four exiting types:

1. 'Timeless wonders' who have great skills, are still relevant and have no reason to quit.

2. 'Ageing despots' who are reluctant to leave.
3. 'Comeback kids' who return to resurrect their company.
4. 'Graceful exiters' who quit while still ahead, leaving behind a sterling reputation.[98]

Heenan then goes on to share his advice about five exit lessons:

1. know your situation;
2. take risks;
3. build networks;
4. continue to be curious;
5. use instinct to know when to walk away.[99]

The innate human tendency to yearn for what one has left behind is not new. Take the story of King Yayati from the Mahabharata, for instance. He was a fine and successful king who worked hard to succeed. Due to certain dénouements, he was cursed by a holy man to age prematurely. His reprieve from the curse was to persuade one of his sons, a future successor, to swap ages with him. The youngest son agreed. King Yayati enjoyed the fruits of youth all over again. It took Yayati a whole life to realize that not all the food, wealth, women and pleasure in the world can appease a man of uncontrolled senses.

Tenuous Ties

Leadership succession and predecessor exit are two sides of the same coin. The predecessor must think and introspect to choose a successor and exit gracefully. Gone are the days when CEOs could enjoy an affectionate retirement function, have their wonderful qualities and accomplishments enumerated and continue a formal or informal association with their beloved company. It may have

---

[98]Heenan, David A., *Leaving on Top: Graceful Exits for Leaders*, Quercus, 2012.
[99]Ibid.

been possible for the good life to just carry on 50 years ago, but not anymore.

Now, stakeholders demand that a successor should resolve persistent issues, even if it means reopening and reviewing the track record of the predecessor. This causes great angst among employees and observers, if the predecessor enjoyed an exhalted status. They may have done many wonderful things and retired with the perception of being God-like. In such a situation, the past actions of the predecessor being re-evaluated is bound to cause distress. Think of what happened to the CEO of GE Jeff Immelt or to General Motors' (GM) Chairman and CEO Richard Wagoner who resigned under pressure, following a request from the White House.

The #EtTu movement is a manifestation of this trend to review predecessors' actions. As part of this movement, successors retrospectively scrutinize their predecessors. The name of the movement comes from the famous line uttered by Julius Caesar upon being betrayed by his friend Brutus in William Shakespeare's *Julius Caesar*: 'Et tu, Brute (You too, Brutus)?'

As part of this movement, investors want successors to examine the blunders of predecessors and make post facto judgements about the latter's actions. They are not interested in placing blame or witch hunting, they just want corrective action. Regulators, investors, analysts and employees may criticize the past leader's tenure, sometimes castigate past leadership or, in extreme cases involving public matters, even bring the past leader to a court trial. For example, a 70-year-old telecommunication officer of the Indian Administrative Service (IAS) was pulled out of retirement to answer for decisions taken during his tenure, over a decade earlier. This also happened with an IAS officer who served as a coal mining administrator. A former bank chairman's decisions were also reviewed after a decade because some loans given during his tenure had gone sour.

Even the private sector has engaged in retrospective scrutiny. First, a case from Unilever unfolded much like the partnership of tennis champions Roger Federer and Novak Djokovic, who partnered in tennis doubles for Team Europe in 2018 and became the only European pair to lose the match. During the 1990s, Unilever had two competent and talented joint chairmen heading its British and Dutch subsidiaries. Individually, they were arguably the brightest chairmen ever. Yet, this combination of two exceptional leaders produced substandard results for Unilever, causing a drastic restructuring of the way the company had been run for several decades. From the second half of the 1990s till the early years of this millennium, the Indian subsidiary of Unilever went through a tough patch, causing public reports and commentaries about whether a mess had been left for successors to clean up. Second, at P&G the continuing global leadership turmoil led to comments being passed about the decisions and actions of the previous CEOs and their legacy.

Third, at GE retrospective takes on past decisions is a decades-old practice. For instance, Jack Welch was a huge evangelist for performance and meritocracy. Yet, his tenure remains a subject of contemporary commentary, decades after he retired. Present day commentators have judged the legacy of Welch's management style. In fact, business columnist John Gapper writing in the *Financial Times*, expressed his view, 'John Flannery was handed the job of catching the falling knives from Mr Immelt's era. [...] GE is so fragile after nearly four decades of asset shuffling under Mr Immelt and his predecessor Jack Welch.'[100]

Successors bearing the pressure of managing a new company are placed in a precarious position. Most try to protect themselves from investor criticism without directly blaming their predecessors.

---

[100]Gapper, John, 'General Electric Has an Overactive Imagination', *Financial Times*, https://tinyurl.com/29psud6y. Accessed on 10 July 2023.

The situation is delicate and the chances of getting it wrong are quite high. Much of the challenge is centred around the ambiguous relationship between an outgoing and incoming CEO.

Is the Board Accountable for Selecting the CEO?

We would like to state the obvious: the board is accountable for CEO selection. While the nomination committee may manage the process and appoint a head-hunting firm to conduct the search, they do so *on behalf* of the board, which is the final decision-making authority. Hence, directors must engage directly with the head-hunter and the selection committee to assimilate their views. They must feel comfortable with the final recommendation. In our experience, the involvement of the directors is not rigorous enough.

An MIT study conducted in 2000 suggested that CEOs appointed after 1985 are three times more likely to be fired than CEOs appointed earlier.[101] It may well be a sign of changing times, but it is also indicative of the fact that directors must reflect on the current fuzzy ways of selecting CEOs. Directors inadvertently abdicate their responsibility of appointing a CEO to the selection committee. So, it seems a tad bit unfair that when a CEO is fired, the board stays. Directors may consider the following suggestions to effectively select a new CEO.

1. In promoter-driven companies and in PSUs, promoters often communicate directly with the CEO, whereas they should have the discipline to express their views through their board nominees. Even though a director is a promoter–nominee, he should use his judgement while accepting or modifying the views expressed by the

---

[101]Bennis, Warren, and James O'Toole, 'Don't Hire the Wrong CEO', *Harvard Business Review*, 2000, https://tinyurl.com/25dd7xya. Accessed on 10 July 2023.

promoter. Multiple views with contrary instructions can leave a new CEO quite flustered.

2. The board must collectively agree on a clear definition of the leadership skills sought from the CEO. Most boards almost certainly leave out the soft leadership skills they desire, like winning hearts, paying attention to others and embracing diversity. Factors like whether the candidate fits the culture of the organization tend to be inadequately discussed, which later leads to the directors recognizing that the CEO they appointed may be a cultural misfit.

3. The incoming CEO is usually not provided an explicit mandate by a coordinated board. Instead, CEOs are generally exhorted to provide a bold direction and to be their own person, but when they do so it causes discomfort.

4. Boards should delegate, not abdicate, the process of hiring a CEO to the search committee. Assuming an appropriate brief and work plan, they should acquiesce rather than participate in the hiring decision. However, mostly, the process is reduced to the search committee recommending a candidate, and the board merely approving and engaging. Leaders must possess a high level of people skills to influence others. Since this is a nebulous subject, it mostly gets sidelined. Instead, directors look for a potential CEO's track record on the parameters of market capitalization, growth in the product market share or earnings. Many years ago, an iconic Coke CEO Roberto Goizueta was succeeded by his CFO Douglas Ivester. Alas, Ivester, a first-class financial whiz, was emotionally inept and the succession did not work. The story of Richard Thoman, who was ousted in absentia at Xerox is similar.[102]

---

[102]'Xerox: The Downfall', *Bloomberg*, https://tinyurl.com/3cxvkevn. Accessed on 10 July 2023.

5. One-man initiatives and excessive cost of acquisitions are other factors contributing to CEO dismissals. At GE, Jack Welch relentlessly drove a sizeable finance division under one set of conditions. His successor, Jeff Immelt was unable to do the same in a market that had changed dramatically in the new millennium. Immelt was compelled to shut the finance business. However, pressurized to bolster growth, Immelt steered the acquisition of Alstom's power business in 2015 in a $10 billion deal. The acquisition failed to deliver target results, led to write-offs and a $23 billion markdown of assets. Immelt's successor, John Flannery, faced the falling knives. He was eased out in less than a year for not dealing with legacy issues. The board remained; the CEO was out.

Hiring the wrong CEO is very much a board issue, especially in India. Unlike the US, in India ousting a CEO is a blemish on the company. A CEO in India may not even receive an exit package. Therefore, it should be imperative for directors to be far more engaged because they are collectively accountable for successful CEO transitions.

Is the Transition from a CEO to a Chairperson Avoidable?

If a CEO mandates that executives should walk away from the company when they retire, that CEO should do the same. Often, a CEO who has performed well retires from an executive position and becomes the NEC of the same company. Is this a wise or foolish idea? Both sides of this debate are undoubtedly loaded with strong opinions, and there is no clear-cut 'yes' or 'no' answer. It depends on the prevailing conditions at the time, and the precautionary processes put in place. There are some successful examples of such a transition, yet the examples of failures are far more. This is because people's behaviour changes when a CEO, however distinguished, is appointed as the NEC of the same company.

What could be the reasons for the CEO to remain associated with the company, after having completed their executive tenure? This could happen for one of two reasons: first, to mentor the incoming CEO; second, to exercise ownership control. While the human desire to hang around or mentor others is universal, the crux of the matter, poignantly illustrated in the film *About Schmidt*, is that it is highly undesirable for the CEO of a professional company to continue as an NEC.

It should always be the successor's decision to seek the predecessor's counsel. Thus, mentoring does not require a statutory position. Furthermore, why should mentoring be made available only to the CEO's successor? Why not to the successor of the retiring national sales manager or factory manager? By this logic, the company will be full of retired mentors which is clearly undesirable. Thus, retiring CEOs must choose to walk away from the company. This is rigorously practised at HUL, GSK (GlaxoSmithKline), Castrol and other MNCs.

Additionally, if the new CEO has not been groomed by the predecessor until his retirement, it is a grave failure—not only of the predecessor but indeed of the board. They should collectively be rapped on the knuckles for failing. India's private sector banks have been culpable in this regard because successful CEOs behave as though their party will never end. It is good to remember that the prospect of an NEC alters the behaviour of the sitting CEO. They may anyway be prone to falling for the egregious assertions of flatterers that his predecessor was difficult to replace.

The 'Promoter' Is Dead

In most countries, the concept of the promoter—the person who ideated or initiated the formation of the company—is relevant only when the company is founded. Thereafter, the founder or promoter becomes a mere record, even more so after decades have passed. The company is meant to be under the control of a management, overseen by directors acting on behalf of shareholders.

In India, however, a promoter continues forever and is stated in the statutory records. This is ridiculous because the promoter is neither a trustee nor an agent of the company. Being named promoter has a privileged status—for instance, SEBI permits promoters' access to price-sensitive information—but that status is perceived as an obligation by the public. The truth is the concept of the promoter is not relevant any longer.

The legal requirement of naming a promoter may well be a legacy of the managing agent, who used to have rights, income and a privileged position. The family or promoter gets a sense of privilege, even if only illusory—a bit like the head of the joint family. The banks derive psychological comfort by collecting letters of comfort, which are usually meaningless, from the promoter to help secure lending facility for the borrower company. It is non-binding in nature and, therefore, in case the company defaults, there is no tangible recourse for the bank against the promoter. Naming the promoter is a hangover of the licence-permit raj. The media knows whose picture to display with headlines like 'Kapoor-led YES Bank'. In international papers, you will not see headlines like, 'Polman-led Unilever' or 'Jeff Immelt-led GE'. Retaining a promoter coalesces a coherent, though useless, image for the relevant stakeholders and could give rise to some piquant outcomes.

A promoter with a shareholding below 25 per cent is a powerless monarch! Yet, founders—driven by a psychological and philological angle of using this terminology—think they have the right to intervene or interfere in the company because they have a special affection for the company or worse, they are like the mother who birthed the company. The emotion evokes empathy but no sympathy. It is as credible as a biological mother who thinks that she can intervene in the dietary choices or marriage of her 30-year-old son.

A start-up founder arrogantly argued that professional managers are like passengers who get on-and-off the train, whereas promoters are the engine drivers who stay with the train all through the journey. One only needs to think of Jet Airways, Kingfisher, Sahara, Satyam, Ranbaxy, Fortis, Saradha Chit Fund and many other companies with usurious promoters who fattened their foreign accounts through purchase contracts.

In the case of L&T's acquisition of Mindtree, 13 per cent of the shareholders ridiculously assumed that they were the champions of all shareholders just because they were classified as promoters, even two decades after the formation of the company.

In the case of Infosys, a 2 per cent shareholder with promoter status assumed the role of the conscience keeper of a shareholder-elected board. Worse still, when Infosys promoters requested to be delisted from the positions, their requests were denied by the authorities.

Similarly, after the death of YES Bank's co-founder and chairman Ashok Kapur, in the 26/11 terrorist attacks in Mumbai, the company rejected his daughter's demand to be nominated on the board, setting in motion a long-drawn-out court battle. If there was no concept of promoter, the YES Bank imbroglio of Kapoor versus Kapur would not have happened. In another case, the NEC of a major cement corporation has been regarded as its promoter, even though he has sold all his shareholdings. The legal continuation of the concept of a promoter in perpetuity has played out its course. There is merit in abolishing the promoter.

Line of Control

Many a CEO have contended that the prospective successor still requires another two years to be ready, as if the company is attempting to deliver an elephant! No one knows where this magical number of two years comes from, but we have noticed that it is consistently used across numerous businesses. Independent directors should call the bluff by insisting that, if it is essential for the CEO to continue as an NEC, the tenure of that role should be no longer than two years. Some successors may actually have benefitted from their predecessors not being around—be it John Walter at AT&T, Michael Ovitz at Disney, Richard Thoman at Xerox or even Ramesh Sarin at Voltas.

Some companies may want to retain the retiring CEO as chairman, not for mentorship, but to exercise ownership control, which is a different context. In a family business, for instance, the major shareholder may wish to leave the hustle-bustle of company management to an executive while retaining control of the board. The CEO is a person who proves their worth and is trusted, hence becoming the obvious choice for this executive. While both reasons are justifiable, both require some discipline in execution, for which a formal board-level exercise is recommended.

The board needs to determine and clearly establish the line of control (LoC) between the incoming CEO and the outgoing CEO-turned-NEC. If this LoC is violated, the independent directors need to swing into action and hold both the NEC and the new CEO accountable. For instance, Marico Limited, a publicly listed company, creditably drew the LoC when Harsh Mariwala became the NEC of the company. There may be more, but we anticipate a significant increase in the future. Goodbyes are inevitable, but the end of an illustrious career need not be a plunge into an abyss of insignificance.

Cleaning up the Mess

Does a successor have to correct their predecessor's blunders? They certainly do. However, it is important to remember that if it is a disaster, it has probably been caused by several predecessors, not just one person. For example, banks' non-performing assets (NPAs). No predecessor can ever hand over a clean slate to a successor; that is simply not possible in enterprise and entrepreneurship.

As CEO Dara Khosrowshahi admitted when he took over from Uber founder Travis Kalanick: 'My predecessor made mistakes. I am going to make mistakes as well. The fact is that I have inherited a fabulous company with fabulous people.'[103] It does not seem likely for Khosrowshahi to have a light workload for a long time.

The challenge is to clean up quietly, professionally and without blame, the last point being a tough act to pull off. Meg Whitman was appointed CEO of HP in 2011 and survived in that position for four years. Whitman made veiled excuses for the write downs, layoffs and revenue declines by blatantly blaming the actions of her predecessors Léo Apotheker and Mark Hurd.[104] Similarly, in November 2018, Matt Comyn, CEO of the Commonwealth Bank of Australia (CBA), blamed his predecessor, Ian Narev, for wrongful selling of consumer credit insurance.

Regardless of the blame game, the cleaning up is a key part of a CEO's job. It *has* to be done; doing it discreetly is desirable although not essential. It is preferable for the successor to visibly improve the organization early on in his tenure. Mistakes are like stocks. There will always be opening stocks, fresh blunders and closing stocks. Incumbent CEOs must be convinced about the

---

[103]"Uber CEO Dara Khosrowshahi: "I've Got a Ton of Work to Do"", *CBS News*, 6 September 2018, https://tinyurl.com/2b3mxjc9. Accessed on 17 July 2023.
[104]Gopalakrishnan, R., *Crash: Lessons from the Entry and Exit of CEOs*, Penguin Random House India, 2018.

opportunity to do the job at hand and outgoing CEOs' errors should not prevent successors from leading an effective team; even if outgoing CEOs are considered heroes or demigods. Here are some practical recommendations for new CEOs to consider.

1. Listen. Even the echoes from the walls of your organization have much to say, just listen.

2. Do not criticize your predecessor, just correct their blunders. The analyst calls, quarterly results and media routines may pressurize you to make necessary statements within the first few months. Take the hit while making these statements, if needed, and proceed.

3. Square up your perceptions with the principal or promoter director(s). They should not be surprised as far as possible. Seek their guidance if not their understanding to avoid becoming a scapegoat.

4. Your management is familiar with the company, its fault lines and how much time it takes to fix the business. Do not try to be a hero to them. If employees perceive you as superman, you have not done well.

5. Focus on building strong connections within the organization, with your new subordinates, business partners and the management. The employees know what needs to be fixed in the plumbing and wiring of the organization. Often, CEOs are so preoccupied with the stress of dealing with the mess and managing colleagues and board of directors, that they miss out on strengthening the strongest allies who have a solution for the difficulties at hand.

6. Rely on your moral authority in addition to your position in the hierarchy. A company's governance system can function well if it is built on a strong moral foundation. The civil engineering principle is relevant here—poor foundation, wobbly skyscraper.

Doing the Job

As a rule, a successor may take two to three years to resolve inherited problems. This constitutes one-third of a tenure of seven to 10 years, provided the cleaning up is done in a congenial manner.

In this matter, the rules of business and politics are quite different. In Indian politics, successive governments have been blaming their predecessors through shambolic and vituperative public utterances about five major problems—black money, unemployment, farmer issues, health and education. It is sobering to note that these problems had been identified even when the Bombay Plan was written by a group of eight businessmen in 1944, nearly eight decades ago!

Even in the politics of other countries, blaming the predecessor is par for the course. During his first term as president, Barack Obama said at a fundraiser in Atlanta, 'We got here after 10 years of an economic agenda in Washington that was pretty straightforward: You cut taxes for millionaires, you cut rules for special interests, and you cut working folks loose to fend for themselves. That was the philosophy of the last administration and their friends in Congress.'[105]

The blame game playing out in organizations tends to push business boards and investors to act faster. This could help the CEO, given the limited tenure and the infinite expectations pinned on them.

A CEO's tenure goes through four phases: seizing the baton, dealing with issues firmly, envisioning the future and, finally, making their legacy. Most CEOs have a rather limited window to take

---

[105]Obama, Barack, *Public Papers of the Presidents of the United States: Book II July 1 to December 31, 2010*, Federal Register Division, National Archives and Records Service, General Services Administration, 2013.

the reins and deal with issues, given the increasing predecessor overhang, shareholder activism and technological disruption.

It is inevitable for all CEOs to inherit their predecessor's karma, be it a balance sheet of debits, low morale or the wrong skill sets. Managing debit notes sensibly and being seen doing so is a delicate balancing act. During this period, there will, almost certainly, be critique. This is especially true if the predecessor is around in any position of influence—as a chairman, advisor or board director. Shades of this were visible in the cases of Ramesh Sarin at Voltas, who resigned following differences with the company board chairman, or even Vikram Pandit at Citigroup and Carly Fiorina at HP.

Jim Donald, a field-driven operating man from the retail domain, was hired as CEO-designate of Starbucks in 2005. Within 18 months, Chairman Howard Schultz and the board decided that the 40 per cent slide in Starbucks's stock prices between 2005 and 2007 warranted Donald's exit. Imagine the number of Indian CEOs who would be on the exit list if the stock price of their company became the yardstick for their retention.

There is an old joke about the advice that a predecessor gave his successor. The predecessor says, 'I have left you three envelopes in the right drawer. Open them and follow my advice whenever you face a dilemma.' When the successor opens the first one at a difficult moment, it reads, 'Blame the predecessor.' On the next occasion, the slip reads, 'Reorganize the company.' On the third occasion, the envelope says, 'It is time to prepare three envelopes for your successor.'

9

Empathy: A Key Ingredient
of Leadership

E mpathy, a key leadership skill, is the ability to understand
the needs and feelings of others. Long overlooked as a
performance indicator, it is, no doubt, the all-important
ingredient that leaders must get right. It has always been a critical
competency for leaders, but it has gained greater significance
in the aftermath of the Covid-19 pandemic, which unleashed a
global crisis on an unsuspecting populace. People's experience of
stress in their personal lives and workplaces was exacerbated by
the pandemic, as demonstrated by research.

The Seattle-based experience management company Qualtrics
conducted a study in April 2020—involving more than 2,000
employees in Australia, France, Germany, New Zealand, Singapore,
the UK and the US—which revealed the new crisis in mental
health.[106] More than 41 per cent of the respondents stated that
their mental health had declined since the Covid-19 outbreak.

---

[106]'The Other COVID-19 Crisis: Mental Health', *Qualtrics*, 14 April 2020, https://
tinyurl.com/r42du5ea. Accessed on 10 July 2023.

Unemployed people had the highest proportion of mental health declines (48.5 per cent) followed by newly remote workers (44.4 per cent) and then all other employed workers (34.1 per cent). People at all levels of the organization were impacted by a decline in mental health. More than 65 per cent of the people reported higher stress after the Covid-19 outbreak. The study by Qualtrics also found that when leaders were perceived as more empathetic, people reported improved mental health.

Empathy need not be considered a passive, sentimental strategy employed by ageing leaders, but one that comes from a deeper understanding of the multiple stakeholders that a business serves. Empathy enables these stakeholders to deliver superior business results too.

A research study confirmed the role of empathetic workplaces in maintaining the quality of personal lives. As one of the researchers stated, 'What I found in my previous study is that email incivility—this general rudeness over email, whether it's the tone, content or timing of a message—really stresses people out on a daily basis.'[107] Their previous study had revealed that those who received a greater number of negative emails reported more strain at the end of their workday, which could manifest in all sorts of ways—from physical symptoms such as headaches to negative emotions. After more research, one of the researchers stated, 'In this new paper, I found that email incivility has more persistent effects. It's not merely a blip on your workday radar and then you forget about it. It has a cumulative negative effect for both workers and their families.'[108] The researchers also found that when employees received more uncivil emails during the

---

[107]Haun, Verena C., Annika Nübold, and Thomas Rigotti, 'Being Mindful at Work and at Home: A Diary Study on Predictors and Consequences of Domain-Specific Mindfulness', *Journal of Occupational Health Psychology*, Vol. 25, No. 5, pp. 315–29, 2020, https://tinyurl.com/mr2zwwmv. Accessed on 5 July 2023.
[108]Ibid.

work week, they 'transmitted' the stress to their domestic partner over the weekend. As a result, the partner too withdrew from their work the following week.

On a positive note, leaders can make a difference to such situations. It was found that when people felt their leaders were more empathetic, 86 per cent reported they were able to better navigate the demands of their work and life—successfully juggling their personal, family and work obligations—as compared to the 60 per cent of those who perceived less empathy.[109] The study also found that empathetic leaders could make people feel more innovative, drive employee engagement and retention, besides helping them feel more included. Empathetic leaders also sparked feelings of greater empathy in the employees.

Being empathetic goes beyond merely responding to employees during times of crises. Leaders, teams and organizations that create a culture of empathy are more likely to succeed by encouraging more human and equitable interactions and policies at all times. The good news is leaders can cultivate feelings of empathy and demonstrate multiple kinds of empathy by asking the right questions. The three key forms of empathy for leaders have been listed below:

1. **Cognitive empathy:** Such empathy pertains to the mind/ thinking. Leaders can imagine how team members are feeling from their unique perspectives. The question to consider is: What would I *think* if I were in their position?
2. **Affective empathy:** Such empathy pertains to the heart/ feeling. This form of empathy involves leaders feeling concern or similar emotions as their employees. The question here is: How would I *feel* if I were in their position?

---

[109]Thompson, Sarah, 'Empathy Is the Most Important Leadership Skill According to Research', *LinkedIn*, 2 July 2023, https://tinyurl.com/3zrxu57f. Accessed on 17 July 2023.

3. **Behavioural empathy:** This has to do with action/doing. It involves leaders actively listening, wanting to understand more about their employee's feelings, experiences or reactions. (The six ways in which leaders may demonstrate empathy have been discussed in the conclusion of this chapter, see p. 141)

On the negative side, exercising power and authority diminishes the mirror neurons in our brain, which may cause lack of empathy. This affliction has been observed for centuries. Lack of empathy manifests among powerful leaders in the form of them not listening, behaving defensively or even arrogantly. Such leaders often dismiss micro-level issues as stray ones because they are unable to perceive the ground-level situation. Leaders who lack empathy tend to struggle with interpersonal relations, which affects their collaborative skills. Unable to manage uncertain or ambiguous situations, they eventually become ineffective leaders.

Leading with Humility and through Dialogue

These are unpredictable times and uncertainty demands that leaders distribute power and develop mechanisms for consultation and empowerment. Leaders need to have deeper conversations and listen empathetically—three times more than they speak, especially in uncertain times. We've discussed the two important lessons for leaders to follow below.

Listen Empathetically

Lend a kind ear to those with less power. Top leaders spend their life climbing up the greasy pole, but they must get off their perch periodically. Gopal recalls HUL chairmen exemplarily interacting with employees and business associates at the front line. Folklore abounds among HUL alumni about the chairmen's field visits, during which they would listen and seek out field perceptions of problems and solutions. Such meetings, being outside cloistered offices, show the leaders being completely attentive to the frontline workers—empathizing with the teams on the ground to make them feel heard and important. Public leaders do so by meeting common people. Recall how Indira Gandhi, then out of power, was the first politician to visit Belchi, Bihar, to meet the victims of the horrendous atrocities against Dalits in 1977.[110]

Too often, leaders are surrounded by committed acolytes rather than constructive dissenters. Active empathy facilitates deeper connections and meaningful collaboration. Empathy is a skill that is best nurtured by keeping one's agenda aside, and seeking to understand the world from the other's perspective. In uncertain times, empathy greatly helps institutions survive and thrive.

Recall the hugely empathetic and humane leadership displayed by those at Tata Steel during the mayhem following a fire in Jamshedpur in 1989 and at Taj Hotels after the 2008 terrorist attack in Mumbai. Both company leaders demonstrated exemplary empathy and humility. In 1964, then Prime Minister Lal Bahadur Shastri insisted that Dr V. Kurien, who had scripted Amul's success story for milk producers in Gujarat, permit him to stay overnight as an incognito house guest of a Gujarati farmer to observe how the system operated so successfully. Leaders come through as endearingly transparent and even vulnerable in such empathetic contexts, greatly augmenting their connect with people.

Don't Overpromise

To some extent, leaders do sell dreams to their followers. This is important because it energizes, excites and motivates others to follow. However, this exercise should not become a litany

---

[110]Ghose, Sagarika, 'On An Elephant, Indira Gandhi, 60, Arrived In Bihar Village', *NDTV*, 8 July 2017, https://tinyurl.com/3zt47nbw. Accessed on 10 July 2023.

of unfulfilled promises. Fiction motivates people to cooperate by lulling them with magical stories. However, the results that followers expect are more important than the promises made by the leaders.

Leaders need to be realistic about actions, which should be specific, measurable, achievable, relevant and time-targeted (SMART). The SMART approach requires collaboration, openness and outreach. The simplest tasks—empathy, humility and dialogue—taken up by any leadership team during a crisis are among the most endearing part of what they do.

Judging the CEO's Impact

How CEOs tend to get judged as opposed to how they ought to be judged is a paradox. The CEO as an organizational leader is perennially in the limelight and is evaluated on numerical values of key performance indicators. However, the mark left by a CEO on the people and institutions is driven by their soft leadership skills. So, a competent leader devoid of humility or humanity can never last long.

Of course, a CEO should be evaluated based on their impact on company performance; but these metrics are commonly only calculated for the duration of their tenure. However, it is noteworthy that for maybe two to three years after taking charge, a CEO's performance is influenced by the organizational momentum they inherited. Likewise, the CEO's successor inherits the organizational momentum, positive or negative, set by the predecessor before their departure. Thus, reading the performance numbers for the duration of the CEO's tenure gives an imprecise picture of their impact.

The impact of the CEO on people and relationships is also considered important. This is difficult to measure and admittedly subjective. Directors need epistemological information on the

CEO's impact on people. Has the CEO effectively motivated people or has he left them fractious and turbulent? Remember how affectionately people regard superlative institutional leaders—like J.R.D. Tata, Vikram Sarabhai, Ravi Mathai, R.K. Talwar, Keshab Mahindra—well after they have departed from their institutions. In contrast, think of Vijay Mallya or the Singh brothers of Ranbaxy.

Leaders that people can recall with professional respect—who manifest human dignity and emotion, and develop a unique yet humble connection with people—are truly effective. People love a leader who is not afraid to be vulnerable, humane and humble. So, rather than relying only on performance metrics, directors must evaluate CEOs on the way they performed. The directors must check whether they were able to earn people's respect without trampling all over them. Directors must reflect on their soft leadership skills and behaviour.

Intentionally discuss employees' feelings. Then, reflect on what they've shared to make sure you understand it correctly without diverting the conversation to your own experiences.

Prioritize meeting with, and getting to know employees not just as workers but as people.

If an employee or team shares an emotional experience or difficulty, give them the space to fully explain it without interjecting or diverting the conversation.

Don't assume your teams and employees know you care about them. Say it when you feel it: 'I care about you; I'm concerned and I understand how challenging this is.'

In one-on-one interactions, whether in person or virtually, if someone pauses while speaking to you, count to five slowly in your head, give them time to find the right words, indicate that you are listening and that they can keep talking if they wish to.

Pay attention to employees' facial expressions and body language to recognize how they may be feeling; maintain good body posture and eye contact, as culturally appropriate, to show that you are listening and not multitasking.

Figure 1: Six ways for leaders to be empathetic

Source: Van Bommel, Tara, 'The Power of Empathy in Times of Crisis and Beyond', *Catalyst*, https://tinyurl.com/5zdy8ubd. Accessed on 10 July 2023.

10

Wisdom: On Boards and in Leadership

Once, as chairman of a start-up, Gopal had a bruising discussion with the CEO, who had flown first class from the US to Mumbai for what he thought had been an 'essential 15-minute meeting'. This is just a minor example of the many boardroom tiffs that have occurred over the past few years. Upon quiet reflection on such events, one realizes that what company directors owe the most to their boards is wisdom, soaked in judgement, character and humility. Wisdom refers to not just a wise decision but also its proper implementation. Considering how common boardroom debacles have become in the recent years, it is a good time for India Inc. to contemplate how to bring more wisdom to the boardroom.

Constituents of Board Wisdom

Carlos Ghosn was a chairman and CEO of three companies concurrently. As CEO of Renault, in 2001, he forged an alliance with Nissan and assumed simultaneous charge of the company in 2005. In 2016, he also became the chairman of Mitsubishi Motors. Each company remunerated him, but none was aware of his terms with the others. The companies performed superbly, and Ghosn became terrifyingly powerful. He made Vijay Mallya's sixtieth birthday party at Goa appear like a retreat for monks. Renault spent €635,000 in 2014 to throw a Louis XIV-style party for him at Versailles. Ghosn was a business hero who had a dramatic downfall in 2018.[111] Directors ignored signals of this aberration until the crisis took them over.

Although such cases may make one think otherwise, several powerful individuals are not inherently immoral or degraded and can be good people. In fact, ironically enough, Ghosn was known as the 'cost cutter' who employed ruthless tactics to bring his companies to good financial health until power corrupted his mind. In the quagmire of conflicting demands, an individual can feel pushed to act in an aberrant and seemingly immoral way. In such moments of temporary loss of judgement, one needs the crutch of wisdom.

Wisdom is born in the crucible of experience and humility. You cannot be trained to be wise; you must *learn* to be wise. Wisdom comes from failure more than success. A wise person possesses character and judgement that can lead to better outcomes. Let us understand these concepts better.

Character

Author David Brooks in his book, *The Road to Character,* states that we live in an 'I' world rather than a 'we' world.[112] Research demonstrates how social and corporate cultures have shifted over

---

[111]Greimel, Hans, and William Sposato, *Collision Course: Carlos Ghosn and the Culture Wars That Upended an Auto Empire*, Harvard Business Review Press, 2021.
[112]Brooks, David, *The Road to Character*, Random House Publishing Group, 2015.

time—from people regarding themselves with humility in the 1950s to thinking of themselves as the centre of the universe in the new millennium. Brooks then suggests that every person has a 'you (image)' and a 'you (real)'.

The you (image) part is competitive and clamours for self-promotion to show that it is highly regarded, acquiring accolades, advancing and, therefore, better than others. The you (real) witnesses your vulnerabilities. It builds your character by winning against yourself, by focussing on your weaknesses and demanding improvement.

Non-executive directors should be at a life stage when their thinking is dominated more by you (real) rather than you (image). They should be dependable, both ethically and professionally. After all, who can be sure when a board colleague could lose balance!

Judgement

We must recognize that we have the potential to transgress our own standards of morality. Good judgement emanating from managerial experience, active listening and welcoming diverse viewpoints can curb these transgressions.[113] Managerial experience may be function-rich, relationship-rich or domain-rich. Active listening means you argue as though you are right but listen as though you are wrong. Welcoming diverse views is as tough as active listening because leaders have touchy egos; they get accustomed to perfunctory discussions and quick convergence on a decision. Temporary loss of judgement can produce unexpectedly harsh consequences. For instance, the valiant Alexander was gracious to those he defeated. However,

---

[113]Likierman, Andrew, 'The Elements of Good Judgement', *Harvard Business Review*, 2020, https://tinyurl.com/4uefe2d9. Accessed on 10 July 2023; Kouchaki, Maryam, and Isaac H. Smith, 'Building an Ethical Career', *Harvard Business Review*, 2020, https://tinyurl.com/y6jejcfm. Accessed on 10 July 2023.

when Batis (the local chief of Gaza) refused to give up the fight or bend the knee, an infuriated Alexander slaughtered Batis ruthlessly and dragged his body around the city.

Wisdom

Wisdom is born out of explicit knowledge and intuition, which are based on experiences and connections with people. Suspicious, aloof and untrusting leaders may experience difficulty in acquiring and reliably demonstrating their intuition.

Here's our formula for a wise director:

You (real) + Managerial experience + Active listening + Welcoming diverse viewpoints = A wise director

Becoming a wise director is a demanding but worthy aspiration. Remember that a competent director is not necessarily wise. It helps to follow the ground rules to develop wisdom until, with practice, even the first idea one has is rooted in wisdom.

The Test of Morality

There are some ground rules—based on comprehension, competence, compliance and conscience—for those holding the reins of a company. For instance, exercising a board's legal rights, be it to approve an acquisition or dismiss an existing CEO, must meet the test of morality. If a director does not agree with a resolution being passed, they must demonstrate strength of character and not vote. There should also be a clear delineation of roles between the owners, board and management. Board directors should place the interest of the company ahead of themselves or the dominant shareholders. They should not leave the 'final' decision to a family member.

When a leader moves from being CEO to NEC, they must modify their style from directing to observing and advising.

This change demands a conscious effort. Presently, there is some brouhaha around the roles of chairman and CEO being separated. Wisdom suggests that it should not be controversial. However, when neeyat and neeti are not in place, such logical decisions are resisted.

An Ethical Grounding

Leaders must teach their teams business ethics and values by practising them. This might seem counter-intuitive in the context of dramatic governance fiascos at IL&FS, which collapsed due to bad governance decisions leading to cost overruns and loan defaults; YES Bank, which crashed under the weight of bad loans; ICICI Bank, which violated almost the entire rulebook, from laws and conflicts of interest to fiduciary duties and the code of conduct; and CG Power, which buckled under accounting lapses. While there is no denying the monumental ethical blunders made by companies, these incidents only confirm that an ethical grounding needs to be laid out for companies, perhaps from a different source—the boss. We must influence managers during their professional childhood, when their ethical brain is plastic. This is the upcoming challenge.

Competitive advantage, which was based on physical assets throughout the industrial revolution, has shifted to intellectual assets during the information revolution. In our view, it will shift to ethical assets amid the AI revolution, which demands far more data transparency. The future could likely belong to strongly ethical companies.

Research on brain functioning has almost concluded that human memory up to the age of three is virtually nil. From ages three to eight, children remember the emotions but not the facts of their experiences. Regrettably, all those joyful hours that we spend with our grandchildren in the park, teaching them chess, playing cricket and taking them to school will mostly not be remembered. What our grandchildren will remember, however, is our affection—all the hugs, kisses and stories that make their eyes wide with wonder. Until the age of eight, through emotions and stories, children learn values and what is right and wrong. The four principles that most grandparents intuitively deploy are emotional time with the children; osmotic learning through storytelling; early correction of behavioural aberrations and multiple interactive experiences.

We have learnt that similar principles influence the ethics of young business professionals. They are not just about inner morality but also about sharing, caring and respecting. Young professionals must be influenced during their training years in business schools, and in the early years of their career. As discussed, their ethical brain is plastic and malleable at this stage. Some corporate entities train freshers through 'ethical experience'. Here are five disproportionately value-enhancing experiences.

1. **Mentoring:** At Abhyudaya—a non-classroom learning initiative hosted by the SPJIMR—every MBA (master of business administration) student compulsorily mentors disadvantaged children as part of the course. While they may not appreciate this experience as students, they treasure it later.

2. **Rural development projects:** Hindustan Lever Limited (HLL) pioneered the idea that every trainee should spend eight weeks living with a family in a village. Every trainee goes through the experience, and leaders honed at HLL are all alumni of HLL's mandatory rural development stint.

3. **Social service projects:** The Tata group introduced eight weeks of social service for every Tata Administrative Service (TAS) trainee. The trainees may not have enjoyed

the experience, but it must have been enriching for them.

4. **Sustainability**: Ethics are not just about honesty and integrity; they are also about respecting our fellow beings and the environment. To this end, sustainability was introduced as a key theme of the Tata Business Excellence Model (TBEM) assessment processes in mid-2000s.

5. **Tone at the top**: Children are sensitive observers of adults' behaviour, and this is true of truth-telling and responses to injustice. Likewise, young managers do what their seniors' do rather than what they say. Everyone at Tata received a salutary lesson on ethics when Ratan Tata blew the whistle on the company, Tata Finance, in the face of financial fraud.

Thus, lessons on ethics, something broader than just having integrity, can be imparted even though it is difficult to teach. It can be done by deploying the same principles that work in a family.

That lack of ethics and morality is distributed in the same proportion among businesses as in media, politics, judiciary, administration, religion and NGOs. Business leaders have also increasingly realized that reputation matters. Everyone from employees to customers respond to good ethics with loyalty and engagement.

Fallout of Leadership Disputes

Even in successful companies, visible and acrimonious leadership disputes can linger—like in L'Oréal, Viacom, Raymond, Infosys, Tata, Indigo and, recently, the Murugappa Group.

We do not judge who is right in a leaders' dispute. It merely emphasizes the obvious: lasting negative consequences linger when a disagreement lands up in the court rather than being negotiated away from public gaze. Inevitably, dust is kicked up by both parties. They both feel that they have contributed to the company although there is usually an asymmetry in their respective perception of their quantum of contributions. Busy lawyers argue in the courts about clauses in agreements or the articles of association. It becomes a dirty debacle.

Commercial disputes, which are usually about money, are inevitable; but leadership disputes, which are usually about ego, are not. A story from John Bunyan's *The Pilgrim's Progress* is relevant in this context. In the story, an interpreter leads the pilgrim Christian into a dusty parlour. The interpreter requests the parlour attendant to sweep the parlour. There is such a thick cloud of dust in the parlour that the Christian can barely breathe. Subsequently, a woman sprinkles water on the dust and sweeps the room clean. The interpreter accompanying the Christian explains his perspective that the dust represents the sin of a person, while the attendant raking up the dust is the law. Law does not cleanse the sin, rather it rouses it further without the power to subdue it. The woman who sprinkles water and sweeps the parlour clean is the gospel.[114] Now this is anecdotal wisdom at its best!

Leadership disputes tend to be about rights and legacy, with a side of ego. No doubt these disputes are quite different from say, a couple's disputes. However, there is some similarity insofar as the disputants have a close working relationship, know a lot of internal secrets and must be sensitive to multiple stakeholders beyond the company.

When a couple decides to separate acrimoniously, friends, extended family and children are involved. Psychological studies suggest that messy divorces adversely affect the parent–child relationship. The child experiences a loss of support at home, and the child's ability to trust the parents gets impaired. Let us look at some examples of some such fraught couples' disputes

---

[114]Bunyan, John, *The Pilgrim's Progress*, Penguin Books Limited, 2008.

affecting children, as depicted in popular movies. These can also be lessons for corporate leaders navigating a dispute before their employees and other stakeholders.

1. In *Parent Trap*, each parent tries to do what they consider best for the children. Their actions end up separating the siblings. In their innocent world, children prefer to see a win–win outcome, where their parents talk to and are civil with each other.

2. In *Kramer vs. Kramer*, the son is torn between his parents in a heart-rending manner. The film points out that it is wrong for either parent to assume what they want is the same as what their child wants. If each parent seeks a win–lose outcome, the child is the one facing a lose–lose dilemma. In such a situation, the child is likely to feel a huge sense of loss.

3. *Mrs Doubtfire* combines humour with a deep message that divorce scars the child, and that parents should find a mutually acceptable solution without public mud-slinging to avoid harming the child.

4. In *The Squid and the Whale*, a successful novelist and his wife agree to separate, but there are two sons involved. As the divorce gets messier, the two sons are pitted against each other, a situation that leads to devastating outcomes for the brothers.

Company leadership disputes and their fallouts are not too different. Such disputes involve vital stakeholders—minority shareholders, business partners and employees—who watch aghast as private matters are made public through court proceedings. In such a situation, the disputants should empathize with the firm's highly engaged employees, many of whom may have served the firm for long and may be loyal to it. Such employees, distracted by public reports, feel alienated from the leaders, whose leadership they might have experienced at work. The disputants should think of the damage to long-standing relations built by employees, vendors, customers and distributors.

However, warring leaders tend to play to win and make it a win–lose game. Other stakeholders perceive the situation to have a lose–lose outcome for them. The lesson is self-evident: disputants should consciously shed their ego. By seriously considering the damage to corporate reputation, the disputants should find a way, directly or through well-wishers, to arrive at a negotiated compromise.

Although competitiveness and spite are endemic to the corporate world, it is better to find it in oneself to forget and forgive rather than to dwell on past disputes. Let us look at an example from Angelina Jolie's 2017 film *Unbroken*. It depicts Louis Zamperini, an American Olympic athlete and Second World War veteran, who suffered severe torture when he was captured by the Japanese. In an interview with *The Atlantic* in 2014, just before his death at 97, Zamperini reflected that forgiving the Japanese had been healing for him. To hate somebody hurts physically, mentally and emotionally. He had quoted Mark Twain, 'Forgiveness is the fragrance that the violet sheds on the heels that crushed it.'[115] Similarly, families and partners with business disputes should subdue their anger through the art of mediation and forgiveness.

Silent Volcano of the 'Trapped' Investor

In business, there are two kinds of investors—direct and inherited. Venture and private equity (PE) firms are direct investors in unlisted Indian companies. Such equity providers,

---

[115]Meroney, John, '"World War II Isn't Over": Talking to Unbroken Veteran Louis Zamperini', *The Atlantic*, 9 November 2014, https://tinyurl.com/49hemam6. Accessed on 11 July 2023.

being professional, secure directorships and legal provisions for an exit. The successful investment of Warburg Pincus in the start-up Bharti Airtel, during the late 1990s, is a classic and happy case study. Pincus exited the investment in 2004, following the company's IPO (initial public offering) when the company was firmly on its feet. In unhappy cases, however, the exit becomes difficult because the company is floundering and not IPO-ready.

The inherited investor, who becomes an heir to stock investments after the death of the giver, can feel trapped. Inherited shareholders may face restrictions on exit and may not have access to the company's finances due to a non-executive directorship. The grievance of a trapped investor can only be alleviated by the majority shareholders, failing which unintended consequences follow.

The dispute of YES Bank's shareholders is an example of trapped investors. After the death of founder Ashok Kapur, his family members did not get a board position despite being substantial shareholders. Another such case is that of a Tamil Nadu-based unlisted, public incorporated company owned by different branches of one family. Their holding company owned an influential percentage of shares in the listed companies of a prominent business group. Upon the death of a major shareholder in the company, his daughters inherited a respectable and valuable shareholding in the unlisted company. However, when the ladies sought a non-executive position on the company board, they were denied. Thus, despite being major inherited shareholders, they were trapped investors. They neither had a satisfactory exit nor any say in the company.

Individuals or companies may become trapped inherited investors. If a publicly listed company becomes a trapped investor, it is a complex situation to solve. Having a dialogue with the majority shareholder of the company and persuading them are the best ways to address the trapped investor's problems. Mediation can be the second stage. Legal action can also be a possibility, although the success rate and time frame involved make it a distinctly unattractive route.

The trapped investor must keep a direct or indirect dialogue alive, and never walk away from the discussion table. As is the case in war-like situations, foreign relations are delicate and it is essential to stay connected, discuss options and compromise within one's limits. Recall the historic and hugely impactful Camp David peace accord between Egypt and Israel. Egypt's surprise Yom Kippur attack on Israel was mounted to compel Israel to return to the peace table. The approach becomes what James Carse termed 'an infinite game'[116], which constitutes a play with no clear rules and no defined beginning or end. If persuasion and mediation fail, the trapped investor may fight ferociously, like a trapped animal.

Nature provides gory lessons on what happens when two similarly resourced animals, like a tiger and lion, fight. The fierceness of the fight hurts both animals gruesomely. Psychologists point out that when trapped, the thinking part of the human brain yields to its emotional part. The trapped investor may inflict severe and unintended harm on the company as witnessed in bitter family business feuds, a highly undesirable situation for both the trapped investor and the company. In a public fight, the issue subtly shifts from business issues to the leaders' egos. The corporate entity, its employees and consumers all suffer in such vicious shareholder battles—just like in wars where the common people suffer the most. Only communication and diplomacy have the power to avert such wars and sustain peace.

The golden rule, derived from experience and prudence, is to embrace diplomacy and dialogue, shunning PR (public relations) disasters and uncertain legal battles. Not following this simple rule can have dire consequences. Driven by either anger or ego,

---

[116]Carse, James, *Finite and Infinite Games*, Ballantine Books, 1997.

one should be prepared to face incalculable damage—both direct and collateral—when the volcano of the trapped investor erupts. Wisdom lies in learning from such failures.

How to Improve Board Dynamics

Numerous factors contribute to a board making unwise decisions. For instance, a momentous and negative shift in a leader's life—a separation, divorce, death of a loved one—may make him a loner or prone to substance abuse. In such a vulnerable situation, he may not listen to anybody or get preoccupied with legacy, which may lead to a governance mishap. If directors can learn to use their long experience and collective wisdom to recognize the precursors to such behavioural aberrations, crises like these could be averted.

The current discourse, however, disproportionately emphasizes rules, procedures and tick-the-box routines by committees and regulators. We argue that apart from such perfunctory procedures, we need to think about and train directors' behavioural aspects for effective corporate governance. There is a compelling case to heighten and deploy judgement and natural intelligence. Perhaps, in the future, artificial intelligence may even help with predictions based on a leader's behaviour. In his work, Gopal often sees companies that really want better board outcomes. While principles of social dynamics help, their application in corporate governance is underdeveloped as yet.

Remember the HST mishap? A flaw in a mirror of the telescope affecting its image clarity was discovered after it was launched into space. This defeated its purpose as an observatory. Clearly, NASA's engineers had focussed too much on the technical aspects of the project and failed to notice, let alone manage, the team's social context, which could have helped detect the fault.

However, even powerful people display signs of behavioural aberrations, as evidenced in the governance failures at WPP. Senior members of the company's team faced allegations of misconduct, like leaking client information to the media. There was also the Thomas Middelhoff case involving embezzlement and tax evasion. Indeed, governance failures in Indian companies—like Religare, YES Bank and ICICI Bank—also had behavioural precursors. The aberrant signals were noticed, but directors felt hesitant to recognize and act on them.

After every episode of corporate governance failure, there is soul searching coupled with considerable bashing of independent directors. Wise corporate governance requires adoption of system-oriented improvement to minimize risk and incidence of such mishaps. Experience with safety teaches us that while its technical aspects are critically important, behavioural aspects are also immensely important. The acclaimed DuPont safety system, a systematic process to identify and evaluate hazards and risks, strongly emphasizes behaviour training. It is the same with corporate governance. Wisdom lies in alertness and action.

Who Is a Wise Board Director?

Corporations need wise directors, but long years of experience do not guarantee wisdom. Just like a muscle, wisdom must be recognized, practised and consciously improved.

The Wise Advocate[117] describes the 'inner voice of strategic leadership', and sheds light on what wisdom is. The book brings together neuroscience, psychology and good writing to explain the brain processes that promote wisdom. It refers to low-ground or fast, transactional thinking; and high-ground or slow strategic thinking. These categories approximately conform to Daniel Kahneman's System I thinking, which is quick and requires no

---

[117]Kleiner, Art, Josie Thomson, and Jeffrey Schwartz, *The Wise Advocate: The Inner Voice of Strategic Leadership*, Columbia Business School Publishing, 2019.

effort, and System 2 thinking which is attentive and effortful. The expressions 'low' and 'high' are not a judgement of quality, rather they denote the location of the brain circuit as you stand erect. The 'low' takes place at a lower ventral level while 'high' takes place in the dorsal or higher point of the brain.

Our first response to a situation or problem emanates from the lower transactional level. Higher strategic thinking kicks in after deep reflection and analysis, and modifies the low-ground perspective through two skills: mindfulness, which involves reflection and analysis; and mentalizing, which involves feeling how the other person feels. Mindfulness and mentalizing are important attributes of the strategic thinking process.

During the late 1980s, for instance, employees at Unilever's tea estate in Doom Dooma, Assam, faced a deadly crisis. A local militant outfit threatened dire consequences if the company did not pay to run its business. Unilever's polite refusal would have had consequences. To avert any harm that could befall its employees, the HUL board dramatically airlifted them and their families from Doom Dooma. That action was based on high-ground thinking.

Another example of high-ground thinking is that of Tata Chemicals. For decades, the company had been seeking natural soda ash to augment its production of synthetic soda ash. In the early 2000s, the Tanzanian government offered a project to mine natural soda ash from Lake Natron. Company directors enthusiastically authorized the management to explore the opportunity. However, after spending several million dollars over five years, the management and board stumbled on the possibility that mining Lake Natron could affect an endangered bird called little flamingo. Applying the precautionary principle, the board canned the project.

Behavioural training assists high-ground thinking. Wisdom is born out of controlling low-ground thinking, with the discipline of high-ground thinking. The mind can be like a noisy and restless engine while the intellect is like the transmission system that smoothly guides the energy to the wheels.

Remarkably, neurological research has now proven something that Vedanta had deduced centuries ago. The human mind is the seat of impulsive and emotional thoughts while the human intellect is the seat of rational and reflective thoughts. Vedanta advises that the intellect should control the mind. Swami A. Parthasarathy, in his book, explains how to practice this wisdom.[118]

Every aspiring director should be trained to be wise. Perhaps, the organizers of courses for board directors could add a valuable session on wisdom.

All Boards are Equal

We urge directors to read *On Board: The Insider's Guide to Surviving Life in the Boardroom*[119], which suggests that board membership is so perilous that one needs advice on how to survive it. With increasing fiduciary accountability of board members, this is partly true. The book is focussed on not-for-profit boards of organizations, like museums and art galleries. Regardless, it serves as a guide, even to commercial boards, on how to navigate the challenges of serving on a board and how governing boards should work.

There is one view that corporate directors are unsuitable to serve on non-profit boards.[120] Non-profit boards are easier to navigate, though different from business boards. Former CEO of British Petroleum (BP), John Brown, and Marks & Spencer's (M&S) director, David Norgrove, have disabused people of this impression. Brown states that the British Museum was a lot more complex

---

[118]A. Parthasarathy, *Governing Business & Relationships*, A. Parthasarathy, 2014.

[119]Tusa, John, *On Board: The Insider's Guide to Surviving Life in the Boardroom*, Bloomsbury Publishing, 2020.

[120]Bowen, William G., 'When a Business Leader Joins a Nonprofit Board', *Harvard Business Review*, 1994, https://tinyurl.com/m9nxt5fr. Accessed on 11 July 2023.

than running a business with an equivalent turnover because of the layers of complexity that go into running a museum. Gopal attests to this from his own experience of serving as a member of a housing society, club and chamber of commerce. He is of the opinion that these roles can be more complex than running a business board.

However, there is a universal way to run a board—one that is common to both companies and non-profits. *On Board* illustrates this through real-life cases, like the British Museum. The author, John Tusa was the MD of Barbican Centre when he was invited to join as a trustee of the British Museum. The museum was set up by an Act of Parliament in 1753. Of the 25 trustees, 15 were appointed by the government, four belong to learned societies, five to the board and, of course, there was the Queen. The reader can imagine how archaic the board must be! Tusa soon realized that the museum was running a £6 million deficit and that the scholarly departments, the heart of the Museum's existence, had become baronies. 'It was time to make the BM's governance work in a way that was true to its past but suited to the complexities of the museum world of the new millennium,' Tusa wrote.[121]

By 2005, the trustees attracted a hugely talented Executive Director Neil MacGregor and Niall Fitzgerald (former chairman of Unilever) to chair the Museum's board. The book narrates how two powerful leaders, with complementary skill sets, established an outstanding working relationship that greatly benefitted the institution.

Some of Tusa's reflections related to governance deserve a mention. He wrote, 'Good governance depends on good behaviour. [...] Governance is an entirely human activity. Those with direct interest in an institution should not, as a matter of law and

---

[121]Tusa, John, *On Board: The Insider's Guide to Surviving Life in the Boardroom*, Bloomsbury Publishing, 2020.

propriety, be involved in supervising its affairs. The ruling principle of good governance is that effective supervision and scrutiny can only come from those without a material interest in the results.'[122]

Tusa also reflected that all board members are equal. If board members wonder what is in it for them, the answer is nothing except the odd free museum ticket or board dinner. Boards do not run the organization—that is the executives' job. That being said, boards should not be kept in the dark and only provided with basic information.

These reflections apply equally to business and non-profit boards. The agenda and context of a non-executive board involves, 'the human interplay, the rows and rivalries, the interactive psychology of behaviour among colleagues, the costs and consequences, the career casualties of board failures, whether caused by indecision, incompetence, misunderstanding, inadvertence or just plain simple rivalry'.[123]

The subject of governance has acquired centrality since the new millennium. The subject is perceived as technical, connecting the three dots of accounting, legal and regulatory departments. Unsurprisingly, in the field of governance, thought leadership has been dominated by accountants, lawyers and company secretaries, who add great value.

A fourth dot, the element of human behaviour, is sorely missing in the discussions about governance. As every director or trustee has experienced, human foibles dominate board functioning—ego, rivalry or treating the appointment as a cherished and prestigious privilege. Thus, it is time for corporate governance to be reoriented to account for societal cultures and human behavioural predilections. This happens when practitioners are willing to write and discuss real-life experiences, potentially

---

[122]Ibid.
[123]Ibid.

leading to a new stream of behavioural corporate governance. Tusa's book may be the harbinger of such a movement.

Emerging Role of Future Boards

Board directors have two distinct roles: that of a map and that of a compass. The former is the traditional role. It is about overseeing the short-term targets within the horizon of a few years. The latter is more about the long-term, securing the future of the company over decades. The role of overseeing is written about most often, although there has been a shift in focus from short-term to long-term.

Management needs new ways of thinking to ensure that businesses survive, expand over the long-term and are sustainable in every sense of the word. Sustainability is about conducting business in such a manner that it can flourish for many decades by being of, for and by the communities around the business.

When we raise our children, we undertake the travails of their infancy and childhood. We also concurrently impart the foundations of human values for their adult years because the short- and long-term are intuitively woven together. We don't think, 'Let us deal with the child's character building later.' Similarly, sustainability should also be built into a company right from its infancy. Nature instructs us that a species is in harmony with its ecosystem when it gives back about as much as it takes. For instance, the coexistence of the Australian possum and the eucalyptus tree. Similarly, team sports teaches us that a winning team consists of collectively collaborative players, who are individually competitive.

In the 1890s, when Jamsetji Tata planned to set up an Indian steel factory and build a 'steel city' around it, he instructed his son, 'Be sure to lay wide streets planted with shady trees, every other of a quick-growing variety. [...] Reserve large areas for football, hockey and parks.'[124] These are the ideas on which the model city of Jamshedpur was built. The story of Jamshedpur is quite similar to that of the Lever brothers. William Hesketh Lever and James Darcy Lever set up the colony township of Port Sunlight, at Merseyside, near Chester, England. It was said of William Hesketh Lever that, 'the ruling passion of his life was not money or even power, but the desire to increase human well-being by substituting the profitable for the valueless'.[125]

There are two lessons to be learnt from these examples. First, sustainability is not an incidental by-product of business. Second, entrepreneurs should think about sustainability early on in the development of the venture. Lessons in sustainability are like yoga and ikigai. Yoga teaches that scientific breathing is not just something we should do because it is 'nice'. We should do it because it is the essence of good living. Simialrly, ikigai teaches that *harahachibu*—eating only up to three quarters of the stomach's capacity—is key to a healthy life.

We may be pardoned for our admiration of Unilever and Tata because, indeed, both deserve it—HUL, as India's most multinational-local company, and Tata Group, as India's most local–multinational group. We know every sinew and vein in these two corporations. Over many decades, both businesses have had a philosophy and heritage of sustainability. Both HUL and Tata are more than a century old; yet, both are youthful and vibrant. In our view, this is because of their sustainability philosophies, which manifest through various terminologies—from corporate social responsibility to environmental impact and community development.

---

[124]Jaywant, Dipa, 'What's So Special About Tata Steel and Jamshedpur?', *India Today*, 9 December 2014, https://tinyurl.com/5n6cbneh. Accessed on 11 July 2023.

[125]Gopalakrishnan, R., 'The Power of Simple and Consistent Purpose', *The Economic Times*, 30 March 2009, https://tinyurl.com/ewmdak4e. Accessed on 11 July 2023.

In this context, it also is worthwhile to remember Castrol India—a fine and long-surviving company that also places sustainability at the core of business. That said, sustainability is not the preserve of century-old companies. Hemas Holdings PLC, Sri Lanka, is a family-owned but professionally run company. This young, publicly listed company operates a programme called *Abhimana* (pride), 'to promote sustainability as a lifestyle across the company,' as demonstrated by their board and management practices.[126]

The boards of such companies agree on time-bound sustainability goals with the management. They leave the execution to the management, which is directly accountable to the board. It is essential, indeed satisfying, for directors to have pre-planned discussions on diverse subjects—like community skill enhancement, promotion of health and education, carbon footprint and water balance—at board meetings.

It is instructive to recall the words of a long-serving chairman of Tata Sons, J.R.D. Tata, 'Corporate enterprises must be managed not merely in the interests of their owners, but equally in those of their employees, of the consumers of their products, of the local community, and finally of the country as a whole.' [127]

The Gyroscope of Governance

Corporate governance depends on checks and balances divided between four institutions: board, management, stakeholders and regulators. It is similar to the democratic political governance depending on the four estates of legislature, executive, judiciary and media. Governance functions like a gyroscope, wherein

---

[126]*Hemas Holdings PLC l Annual Report 2018/19*, 2018, https://tinyurl.com/mvvhmdh6. Accessed on 5 July 2023.
[127]Lala, R.M., *Beyond the Last Blue Mountain*, Viking, 1992.

excessive swings along some axes can be balanced out by effective institutions. The gyroscope is free to rotate in many directions, while its rotor maintains the spin axis and orientation. The design and functioning of a gyroscope are key to engineering applications, like the mounting of the HST. Similarly, if any of the four estates of political or corporate governance flounder and other institutions are unable to bear the pressure, there are consequences.

The 2020 US elections created waves of shock and disbelief across the world, when unstable leadership surrounded by fawning myrmidons almost wrecked a two-century old system. Since 2016, the US media had been reporting on the five messages being drilled into people—stop appeasing the 'others' who are 'not like us'; wrest influence away from experts; ally with global leaders who think similarly; pursue nationalistic self-reliance; and wish for the glorious past. These messages were packaged as a self-eulogy about the 'unparalleled and historic accomplishments', which further bolstered the image of the leader's invincibility. Such dangerous political and corporate leadership is also visible in other nations.

Lessons from political governance can be instructive for corporates. According to Professor Dacher Keltner, leaders continue to fail because 'power damages the leader's brain and diminishes the very emotional capacity of empathy that helped the leader to rise in the first place'.[128] Under such circumstances, checks and balances generally work. Recall how the Indian electorate rejected Emergency in 1977 or voted out a smug government in 2004. In both cases, a credible alternative had not been in sight, yet the voters had acted.

Of course, sometimes, the gyroscope fails when the balance between the four institutions—board, management, stakeholders

---

[128]Gopalakrishnan, R., *Crash: Lessons from the Entry and Exit of CEOs*, Penguin Random House India, 2018.

and regulators—is shaken. This is evident in some of the corporate examples discussed below.

The first example is of Air India—an airline that started in 1932 and became world-class by the 1950s. Then, it received its first blow when it was nationalized. J.R.D. Tata wrote at that time, 'Even more than the decision itself, I was upset by the manner in which nationalisation was introduced through the back door without any consultation...'[129] The second blow came in 1978, when J.R.D. Tata was unceremoniously removed as chairman of Air India. The corporate gyroscope creaked for years while the organization was decimated by succeeding governments. There was little governance because the four institutions all coalesced into one.

The second example is of the rise and fall of GE, as commented upon by Thomas Gryta in *Lights Out*. Jeff Immelt, successor to the legendary Jack Welch, selected Beth Comstock, a media relations executive, to be his chief marketing officer in 2003. GE instructed its leaders to have a story behind every initiative, with Comstock arguing, 'story is strategy'. Sound strategy is enhanced by a good story, but a good story cannot substitute sound strategy. The directors watched the share prices slipping year after year for 15 years before making important CEO changes. The current leadership now faces an uphill task of rebuilding the company to its past glory.

The third example is the emergence of Nestle India from the tangle of the controversies surrounding Maggi noodles. After early missteps, a determined management and a strong board overcame a crisis of consumer confidence arising from a regulatory intervention. At one stage, it appeared catastrophic but the checks and balances worked.

The final example is of an arrogant CEO and a powerful American company, Montgomery Ward. In the war-torn US of

---

[129]'Sly Takeover of Air-India Hurt JRD', *Rediff.com,* 4 August 2004, https://tinyurl.com/55cuavjv. Accessed on 11 July 2023.

1944, the company supplied several war-time essentials. However, supply had been disrupted due to labour union disputes. The company chairman Sewell Avery refused to settle the strike, thus endangering the delivery of essential goods. Upon being nudged by President Roosevelt, the War Labour Board intervened. Avery blustered and stormed, while evading questions, and was incensed enough to state, 'War Labour Board must be destroyed, and this is no way to build a successful country.'[130] Astonishingly, President Roosevelt ordered the army to take over the company, but Avery still did not relent. As captured in a memorable photograph by *TIME*, the army physically carried out the chairman from his office.

Clearly, power can lead to megalomania and the consequent brain impairment can reach extraordinary levels.

Resistance to Diversity

In April 2020, Abigail Disney, granddaughter of the legendary Walt Disney, chided the Disney board for reducing the pay of workers while protecting executive pay by saying, '...pay the people who make the magic happen with respect and dignity they have more than earned from you.'[131] In March 2021, McKinsey & Company published an article that stated that Hollywood could increase its revenues by $10 billion each year if only it would promote more diversity.[132]

---

[130]'Sewell Avery', *Google Arts and Culture*, https://tinyurl.com/vp2zcchb. Accessed on 5 July 2023.

[131]Sinha, Charu, 'Abigail Disney Criticizes Walt Disney Company Slashing Worker Pay', *Vulture*, 22 April 2022, https://tinyurl.com/35bjmne3. Accessed on 11 July 2023.

[132]Dunn, Jonsthan (et al.), 'Black Representation in Film and TV: The Challenges and Impact of Increasing Diversity', *McKinsey & Company*, 11 March 2012, https://tinyurl.com/38wmz4v9. Accessed on 5 July 2023.

We write about diversity with an emphasis on board gender diversity. Boards tend to favour the creation and perpetuation of a homogenous whole. Nomination committees seek a director who will 'fit in'. Through the existing practice, diversity becomes a casualty—by gender, linguistic group or nationality—because, according to the current definition, diversity means a person who is *not* like the others.

While there are evolutionary and social factors, there is also a neuropsychological factor to diversity. Psychologist and neuroscientist Dr Lisa Feldman Barrett recently wrote in *The Guardian* that variation places an additional burden on neurons by demanding more resources.[133] Another learning from Dr Barrett is that the principal function of the brain is *not* to think or to learn new things, but to monitor and keep all the systems of the body working. To do this, the brain tracks resources, like glucose, salt and water, through a process called allostasis. When confronted with unexpected experiences, the allostasis of the brain alters. The brain discomfort increases further if there is a tense environment (as may happen at a board meeting). The brain and the body do adjust, but discomfort as a metabolic response is inevitable.

Although the brain resists variation, it is at the core of the evolution of life forms. Embracing differences is vital for success as a species. Charles Darwin's theory of survival of the fittest confirms that variation is essential, not just desirable. Without variation, a species can go extinct. If company boards or citizens of a nation do not welcome variation, their eventual homogeneity can pose an existential threat. This can be seen through corporate experience and history.

---

[133]Feldman Barrett, Lisa, 'The Big Idea: Do Animals Have Emotions?', *The Guardian*, 29 August 2022, https://tinyurl.com/2wytw9k6. Accessed on 5 July 2023.

A 2015 McKinsey report stated that companies with more diverse workforces perform better financially.[134] More diversity means more perspectives, which enriches the organizational response to unexpected crises and events. Gopal experienced this as the chairman of Unilever Arabia, working with people of 16 nationalities. Indeed, the energy and vigour of Unilever globally owes a lot to employee diversity.

In a personal conversation with Gopal, Suresh Narayanan, chairman of Nestle India, recounted how, at the peak of the Maggi noodles crisis, his HR head had said, 'You are doing dipstick opinion surveys and talking to government. How about engaging with our own employees?' Narayanan credits his large and diverse employee base for several ideas that helped turn the situation around.

History too adduces to this fact. The Ottoman empire was dominated by Turks but also included Arabs, Kurds, Greeks, Armenians and encouraged Christians, Jews and other religions to join. The Ming dynasty in China had cultural and economic ties with many nations. Calicut residents can regale you with stories about how Ming ships arrived there, leaving behind a Silk Street that exists to this day. The Mughal empire was characterized by diversity. In fact, cultural diffusion and acceptance was the hallmark of the early Mughals.

For India, diversity is surely a competitive advantage. So many religions have coexisted harmoniously for centuries here. In our country, you can find Changpa nomads, Animist Santhals, Husseini Brahmins, Siddi Kannadigas, Bene Israeli Maharashtrians, Zoroastrian Parsis, and much more. In short, diversity is in India's DNA—it powers the country's survival and growth.

---

[134]Hunt, Vivian, Dennis Layton, and Sara Prince, 'Why Diversity Matters', *McKinsey & Company*, 1 January 2015, https://tinyurl.com/mr26e82x. Accessed on 11 July 2023.

For corporate boards, diversity is a strategic advantage. Despite its many benefits, we struggle with diversity. To adapt a quote by Mahatma Gandhi to the corporate context, 'I do not want my boards to be walled in on all sides... As soon as we differ from somebody, instead of meeting and understanding him, we ignore him or take him to task publicly.' To fight the urge to otherize people, Dr Barrett recommends meeting, talking and reflecting deeply about why someone you regard well holds an opposing view from yours. Disentangling their logic from emotions helps you appreciate their logic, even if you do not agree with it. We find that this approach works for Mumbai's clubs and co-operative societies, which sometimes seem like a uniquely uncooperative group of people. On a larger canvas, it could do wonders.

Crisis Requires Collaboration, Not Competition

Usually, the leader is the only one who is blamed for failure, just as he is the only one who is credited for success—both are unfair but reflect the reality. Unremarkable leaders take credit and shirk blame. However, it is not the error that defines the leader, but what happens *after* it. Denying a mistake is a terribly diminishing action. Every leader who shirks responsibility sets a bad example for future leaders by being a visible example to the constituency. Acceptance of responsibility contributes to success as a leader. In 1979, for example, the Indian Space Research Organisation's chairman, Satish Dhawan accepted responsibility for the failure of the first SLV-3 rocket launch. At the success of the next launch, he stayed in the background and credited his team.

In 2016, the America's Cup World Series regatta was held in Oman. Sir Ben Ainslie, the most successful Olympic sailor in history, captained a potential winning team sponsored by the

Tata-owned Land Rover. Ainslie misjudged the winds in the first two of the three heats, so he had to allow other boats to pass him. Ainslie humbly accepted the misjudgement and implored his team to help win the third heat, which they did.

Robert Rubin was feted as a hugely successful treasury secretary of the US during the 1990s. He loosened controls on the financial industry during his tenure. The financial bust followed, which led to the loosening of controls being criticized. By 2008, as a senior advisor of Citigroup, he said that nobody had been prepared for this. With the facts that the board had known then, maybe they should have acted differently. There was an enormous amount that needed to be learnt.[135]

Gopal once heard a beleaguered CEO demand of his communications team, 'Only negative stories are appearing. Get out positive stories about our successes please.' The result of the team's efforts was another disaster. Although the boss had got seven out of 10 things right, common people were not interested beyond how the system would fix the three missed pain points.

The price of greatness is responsibility. History teaches us four generic lessons about taking responsibility.

1. Be aware that things are not always as they seem.
2. Accept that admitting failure is not a weakness.
3. Take actions that will make a difference.
4. Actively reach out and build trust.

Conversely, the four missteps to avoid while handling failure are:

1. underplaying problems by comparing them with bigger ones;

---

[135]Brown, Ken, and David Enrich, 'Rubin, Under Fire, Defends His Role at Citi', *The Wall Street Journal*, 29 November 2008, https://tinyurl.com/3dfcp2de. Accessed on 5 July 2023.

2. allowing your supporters to shift the blame;
3. telling misleading half-truths or, worse still, lies;
4. passing the blame to others.

Wisdom is embedded in these simple leadership rules.

PSUs: Include Boards and Exclude the Government

To curb the influence of promoters and empower independent
directors, SEBI introduced new regulations for listed companies.
Several promoter-driven companies do deserve such regulations.
However, it seems to have overlooked the cases where the
government is the promoter. PSUs have been exempted from SEBI
regulations for board governance. Why are they treated like a
special case for applying the Companies Act and SEBI supervision?
Surely the same corporate regulations must apply to them. The
problems faced by PSU management are well researched.

Renewed and transformed business institutions, whether
led by the government, promoters or a professional body, are
strategically important to the national economy to generate the
resources required to enable national investments in health,
education and culture. One of the major reasons for India's
inadequate economic and social progress over the last seven
decades is surely the policy failure to nurture enough sustainable
and honest business institutions. Private sector malfeasance
is written about. PSUs too offer valuable and instructional
narratives. It is time to blow the whistle on unacceptable PSU
performance. This is not a plea to eliminate PSUs, but to run
them more efficiently.

PSUs have played a well-defined role in India's progress
over 75 years. Some have delivered sterling outcomes that the
return-seeking, capital-poor private sector would have been unable
to do. However, tax-paying citizens expect that, at some stage,

PSUs should generate a return on capital, which may be higher than the cost of capital, if not extraordinary. Being a PSU cannot be a licence for poor returns and inefficiency.

It is a pity that political and bureaucratic structures misuse PSUs for their own benefit. As R.C. Bhargava, a bureaucrat turned business leader, wrote:

> PSU managements have not been able to create companies where continuous improvements in productivity and quality takes place [...] because it is the government, and not the management that takes key financial, technological, and commercial decisions. [...] Unlike private sector promoters, ministers and officers have not invested their own money. [...] Creating immense scope for a political party to use PSUs for its own political advantage. [...] Boards make little difference to management quality, and thus a major instrument of corporate governance is blunted.[136]

In his autobiography, former civil aviation secretary, M.K. Kaw, wrote about the aviation industry, 'A fascinating saga of benami ownership. [...] Unwarranted purchase of aircraft, mismanagement by bureaucrats and politicians...'[137]

The Indian public has long been aware of what these authors have merely emphasized. The ugly truth is buried in the commercially irresponsible way in which governments of all hues have supervised and controlled PSUs since Independence. Consider the unfortunate tale of Air India. The company started off as Tata Airlines. Subsequently, it was rather abruptly nationalized while continuing to remain connected with the Tata Group under J.R.D. Tata, until his removal as chairman. Finally, many decades later,

---

[136]Bhargava, R.C., and Seetha, *The Maruti Story: How a Public Sector Company Put India on Wheels*, HarperCollins India, 2010.
[137]Kaw, M.K., *An Outsider Everywhere*, Konarak Publishers, 2012.

after clocking too many losses, the airline was returned to the Tata Group in January 2022. Who is to be held accountable for ravaging the airline? Air India insider and former director, Jitender Bhargava, wondered, 'Do we blame the government [...] or the board [...] or successive chairmen [...] or the union leaders who made unreasonable demands?'[138]

There, of course, are happy exceptions among PSUs, led by strong and competent leaders like V. Krishnamurthy at Bharat Heavy Electricals Limited and D.V. Kapur at National Thermal Power Corporation Limited (NTPC). Kapur described how NTPC built people power by prioritizing recruitment, training and talent density while operationalizing the new company.[139]

Indian energy-sector PSUs—like the Oil and Natural Gas Corporation, Power Grid Corporation of India, Bharat Petroleum Corporation Limited, in addition to NTPC—are much sought after by foreign investors. These are successful probably because of great leaders, sound systems or monopolistic benefits. Surely then, it is possible to set up and run PSUs that are efficient. Why should it be a rare occurrence?

India has been in serious need of better-managed PSUs for at least 30 years. To achieve this goal, the government must stop behaving irresponsibly—like some of the private-sector promoters on whom the government is heaping new regulations. Indian PSUs need to exclude the government and include boards in their structures. This will lead to less government and more governance.

---

[138]Bhargava, Jitender, *The Descent of Air India*, Bloomsbury, 2013.
[139]Kapur, D.V., *The Bloom in the Desert: The Making of NTPC*, HarperCollins India, 2015.

Ideal Tenures

Someone once said, 'Politicians and diapers must be changed often, and for the same reason.' This applies to business leaders as well. Exceptions apart, a healthy CEO tenure is less than 10 years. The American presidency is restricted to two terms. Among Indian prime ministers, Pandit Jawaharlal Nehru, Indira Gandhi, Rajiv Gandhi and Manmohan Singh all started well. After seven years in office, each of them started to lose leadership impact. When leaders linger long, warning signals of reduced effectiveness begin to show, often with increasing intensity.

What about business leaders? Even if powerful leaders have not been effective for a long time, people hesitate to challenge them. Gopal has always emphasized that it is important for a governance professional to recognize and act on ambiguous signals. Problems do not go away. He accordingly proposed a 15-point test for directors, centring on the warning signals of their reduced effectiveness.[140] If directors notice recurring complaints about a leader, they must actively consider what to do. As former CEO and governance expert, Ram Charan wrote, 'Conscientious directors can act in a professional manner by doing two things: speaking up and reaching out.'[141]

For instance, at GM, the leaders reacted positively to such warning signals. John DeLorean, who served GM for 17 years, was a terrific engineer who breathed new life into a staid Pontiac. However, gradually, DeLorean's behaviour became increasingly obsessive and compulsive. Top leadership curtailed his prima donna behaviour, compelling him to quit GM. He then set up DeLorean Motor Company (DMC), where he created interconnected problems

---

[140]Gopalakrishnan, R., 'Leaders Should Be Changed Periodically', *Business Standard*, 10 August 2021, https://tinyurl.com/w2fkc6u6. Accessed on 11 July 2023.
[141]Charan, Ram, *Boards At Work: How Corporate Boards Create Competitive Advantage*, Jossey-Bass, 1998.

relating to financial, drug and social malfeasance, earning him a jail sentence. He died in 2005, aged 80. Netflix has memorialized his story through a film titled *Framing John DeLorean*.

Similarly, at the WPP Group, Martin Sorrell was known to be a powerful bully who was ousted by the board. Following Sorrell's exit, WPP group suffered only minor bruises. In another such case, Thomas Middelhofff, the long-serving CEO of Germany's Bertelsmann, crashed his next company (Arcandor). He was also accused of misusing corporate funds for taking private trips on chartered aircrafts. He, too, served a repentant jail sentence. Similarly, Ravi Narain, the long-serving leader of the National Stock Exchange (NSE), got embroiled in a money laundering case, suffering from hubris and humiliation as written in Debashis Basu and Sucheta Dalal's book, *Absolute Power*.[142]

Metabolically and neurologically, power can cause temporary brain impairment in a leader. We have noticed that it takes some time for such impairment to materialize. It is excessive tenure that leads to absolute authority, usually in the later phase of the leader's tenure. Listed companies that have been effectively run seem to change CEOs with planned regularity: the average tenure of CEOs at HUL is six years; TCS is six years; Titan is 10 years; and at Tata Steel is eight years. Contrast these with the long leadership tenures at IL&FS, NSE and YES Bank. At the fabled GE, Jack Welch's two predecessors had tenures of nine years each, while Welch had 20 years.

According to the annual survey by *Strategy+Business*, the average tenure of CEOs is six and a half years at the world's 2,500 largest companies.[143] Of course, there are notable exceptions, but

---

[142]Dalal, Sucheta, and Debashis Basu, *Absolute Power - Inside Story of the National Stock Exchange's Amazing Success, Leading to Hubris, Regulatory Capture and Algo Scam*, Kensource Information Services LLP., 2021.

[143]Lucier, Chuck, Eric Spiegel, and Rob Schuyt, 'Why CEOs Fall: The Causes and Consequences of Turnover at the Top', *Strategy+Business*, 15 July 2022, https://

sensible company boards should not test the wisdom received on leadership tenure.

Irrational Exuberance and Rational Humility

The disconnect between the fundamentals of several companies and their market valuations has widened over the years. While this exuberance may be justified for a few companies, for most, it will be judged to have been thoroughly misplaced.

Disruption is to be welcomed; it is a fantastic event. History is witness to the fact that there is a thin line between disruption and mania. For instance, in 1636, Tulipomania took over Holland when speculation drove the value of tulip bulbs and led to a market crash. In 1719, the Mississippi bubble triggered a speculative frenzy and led to financial collapse in France in the eighteenth century. In 1720, the South Sea bubble marked the financial collapse of the South Sea Company formed to supply slaves to Spanish America. More recently, Nick Leeson's last few speculative trades brought down the mighty Barings Bank. Corporate raider Gordon Gekko could not have predicted that his protégé, Bud Fox, would betray him. Harshad Mehta's systematic stock scam using fake bank receipts and stamp papers crashed the stock market. All of them served jail terms as did Gopal's former colleague, and former Tata Finance director, Dilip Pendse for whom the world collapsed while he was attempting to cover trades gone horribly wrong.[144]

Things go awry, markets behave unpredictably. Through the disruptions, however, our concern is for the hard-earned savings of middle-class investors, which could be at risk. The odds are decidedly stacked against such investors if the calibre

---

tinyurl.com/bdem5p3s. Accessed on 5 July 2023.

[144]Axelrod, Alan, *Profiles in Folly*, Sterling, 2008.

of the companies getting listed—and the grey market premiums accorded to them—are anything to go by.

Capital market activities impact Indian citizens irrationally, much like cricket does, making them feel sadder or more excited. Unlike cricket, however, capital markets can be cruel and punishing if investors do not check their instincts. Fortunately, there are three simple rules worth following to avoid financial heartburn.

1. Know what you own and where to draw the line while being aware that the power of greed can shake the resolve to follow this rule.
2. Know how much to own, which is a basic rule of thumb when investing in early-stage IPO companies. Invest what you are prepared to lose—an amount that will not negatively impact your lifestyle. Most investors at the height of their mania do just the opposite, hoping to maximize their wealth in the shortest period.
3. Own your decisions. At the end of IPO mania, a post-mortem is always done on what the listing company, the investment bankers, the regulator or even the government could have done to protect small shareholders. The conclusion is always the same: the buck—a euphemism for losses—always stops with the investor, however large or small.

What makes the upcoming IPOs unusual is that many of them defy conventional valuation methodologies. Companies have traditionally been valued on cash generation, successful financial history and distinctive pricing power, which reasonably reflect future earnings growth. Several loss-making companies are valued at billions of dollars. However, they do not generate any cash flow, do not have any history of earnings and lack any modicum of pricing power. Yet, miraculously, they are expected to grow revenues exponentially with a hazy route to cash generation. They are also expected to generate a profit at some point in five years and positive cash flow in 10 years.

The reality is that while a lot has changed over the years, fundamental valuation techniques have not. As the successful entrepreneur Alan Mitz reportedly said, 'Turnover is vanity, profits is sanity, but cash is reality.'[145] This adage reflects the state of valuations and why very few companies live up to expectations. To better understand why, count how many profit-making companies worth more than a billion dollars have been established over the last 15 years? Contrast this with the number of unicorns out there and ask yourself: have business fundamentals changed overnight? What makes investing seem simple to those outside the profession is the perception that there is a 50 per cent chance of success or failure on every investment. You would not say the same about other professions, such as pilots, surgeons, dentists or engineers. Rest assured, investing is not as simple as it seems.

India is a tough place to earn profits. There are about 250 listed companies with a market capitalization of $1 billion or more in India. Several have become profitable only after enduring many tribulations and heartbreaks. At the same time, loss-making start-ups are often valued at over $1 billion, initially through private transactions but lately through public markets. In 2021, India witnessed the birth of 44 unicorns with a total valuation of $93 billion.[146]

India celebrated and welcomed a new unicorn—a $1 billion company—every 10 days! This was sheer ecstasy for a few, but does it signify another bubble followed by a crash and delayed pain for many?

This is best reflected in research published by Professor Hendrik Bessembinder of Arizona State University, which shows

---

[145]'The Power of One | Alan Mintz', *Wonder Podcasts*, https://tinyurl.com/3txjwhk8. Accessed on 5 July 2023.

[146]'The Indian Unicorn Landscape', *Invest India*, https://tinyurl.com/yc2w49fr. Accessed on 17 July 2023.

that from 1926 to 2016, over half of all the net wealth created in the US stock market was created by 90 companies—just 0.3 per cent of all companies.[147] Small investors need to understand the asymmetrical outcomes and probabilities involved in such payoffs.

The only antidote to irrational exuberance is rational humility combined with a deep sense of self-awareness, which helps protect one's wealth, health and happiness.

Companies Need More Neeti, Less Niyam

Warren Buffett has famously blamed 'boardroom atmosphere' for governance failures by otherwise intelligent and decent directors.[148] Boards tend to be part business organizations and part social organizations. Being effective in such an organization may require a director to play politics. Recently, even the director of the SFIO reprimanded independent directors for failing small shareholders.

Although listed companies have three broad classes of shareholders—majority, minority and institutional—the board is required to consider the interest of *all* shareholders, even though each class of shareholders is a constituency by itself.

The majority shareholders, including the promoters, belong to the class of risk-taking entrepreneurs. Like the Marathas, who perceived themselves as risk-taking conquerors, the majority shareholders behave in a clannish manner whenever a dispute arises between one of them, the management or other shareholders. Recall the fight between the Shaw Wallace chairman S.P. Acharya and the Dubai-based entrepreneur Manu Chhabria for the control

---

[147]'Do Stocks Outperform Treasury Bills?', *W. P. Carey School of Business*, https://tinyurl.com/yzt6a2kb. Accessed on 5 July 2023.

[148]Cunningham, Lawrence, 'Warren Buffett's 10 Commandments for Running a Successful Business', *CNBC Make It*, 19 July 2017, https://tinyurl.com/mryfhsxa. Accessed on 11 July 2023.

of the company during the 1980s, or how India Inc. reacted when British businessman Swraj Paul tried to grab control of large, possibly controlling shareholdings in DCM (Delhi Cloth Mills) and Escorts in 1983.

Promoters also tend to behave dynastically. In a public debate in Kolkata, the chairman of a family-run, listed company brazenly asserted, 'This company belongs to my family, I took over from my father, and my son will succeed me. We engage professionals to implement our decisions and to manage.' Does he not sound like a true Maratha, who used to appoint Peshwas to administer conquered territories? Perhaps, he would avoid having independent directors if regulations did not compel him.

Recently, another class of entrepreneurs has emerged—the professional entrepreneurial manager (PEM). Entrepreneurs are rightly thought of as risk takers and professionals are aptly considered process-oriented people. PEMs combine both traits. Think of Prakash Tandon (HLL), Ajit Haksar (ITC) and Champaklal Choksi (Asian Paints). Their actions exemplify that behaving in an entrepreneurial manner is not the preserve of a business family, and an MBA is not a prerequisite for being professional. There are successful companies—like HDFC, L&T and ITC—run by PEMs with no majority shareholder. Occasionally, such CEOs even behave like promoters.

Independent directors, typically retired bureaucrats or professional managers, fall under the class of minority shareholders. Majority shareholders work incredibly hard to get amenable independent directors. Sometimes, an independent director so greatly values prestige and board fees that he feels obliged to support the promoter and management due to an authority bias.

Another class of institutional directors may be nominated by domestic or foreign financial institutions. Domestic nominees play the passive role of watching and stay uninvolved unless a crisis arises. However, foreign nominee directors are professional investors trained in valuation and governance systems. They assertively hold managements up to a high performance standard. Institutional directors are mostly trained to ask tough questions.

Into this melee enter regulators—not one, but multiple. Like the Indian pantheon of gods, multiple regulators intervene with simultaneous jurisdiction, keeping the judicial system busy. The judges of the higher courts are so overburdened with tax, corporate and political disputes that they have inadequate bandwidth to deal with important civic and criminal matters.

Such governance disputes will continue so long as there are self-interested promoters, money-motivated institutional investors, small shareholders and regulators. The key is to train and align directors not only about the laws but also about the behavioural aspects of governance. Companies need more neeti, less niyam.

Constructive Dissonance Helps Good Neeti

Given the current dissonance between promoters, independent directors, management and regulators, institutions need to develop better neeti. Values-driven companies actively encourage constructive dissonance. Institutions without constructive dissonance are like cars without brakes. Future leaders are likely to listen, be empathetic and vulnerable.[149]

Codes of conduct and business principles are necessary but not sufficient. J.R.D. Tata had once rather sarcastically told the Planning Commission in 1968, 'I must be possessed of tremendous economic power. [...] I carefully consider what I should accomplish. Should I crush competitors, exploit consumers, fire recalcitrant

---

[149]Fitzgerald, Jay, 'What Companies Want Most in a CEO: A Good Listener', *Harvard Business School*, 26 October 2021, https://tinyurl.com/5546x544. Accessed on 5 July 2023.

workers, topple a government or two?'[150] He meant to emphasize that, despite the popular narrative, company executives are not constantly scheming to make an illegitimate buck.

Arguably, involuntary fraudsters are leaders like Vijay Mallya and Rajat Gupta. Accused or convicted executives are often unaware that they are committing a crime in the first place, although they are presented as congenial crooks.[151] Malfeasance occurs because of an aberrant judgement by overconfident leaders in institutions where constructive dissonance or presentation of diverse views is absent. A debate on different perspectives will always deliver better results than a unitary decision. Ancient texts are replete with exhortations for followers to listen, reflect on what is said, voice contrarian views and debate opposing viewpoints to arrive at a reasoned opinion. Being immersed in a culture that encourages expression may perhaps account for the volubility of Indians. As the economist Amartya Sen wrote, 'Prolixity in not alien to us in India.' [152] Unlike the canonic teachings, constructive dissonance has always been encouraged in India. It is integral to being a Bharatiya.

India has an extraordinary tradition of constructive dissonance compared with global intellectual philosophies. It is this inheritance that secures adherence to values, morality and complex dilemmas that work as a hidden competitive advantage. It is bewildering to see that high public officials blame colonial mentality, civil society and dignified companies for holding back the nation's progress. Certainly, company managements should preserve it.

Just as there are no perfect human beings, there are no perfect corporates. For instance, *jee-huzoor* companies are dangerous and

---

[150]Lala, R.M., *Beyond the Last Blue Mountain*, Viking, 1992.
[151]Soltes, Eugene, *Why They Do It: Inside the Mind of the White-Collar Criminal*, PublicAffairs, 2016.
[152]Sen, Amartya, *The Argumentative Indian*, Penguin Random House, 2005.

reckless. How do you recognize a values-driven or principled company?

Subject to some inevitable aberrations of behaviour, we have observed that sustainable and ethical companies largely share two characteristics: longevity and maintaining a low profile through financial conservatism. Some companies that practice corporate anonymity include Unilever, Tata, Godrej, Kikkoman and Bosch.

About 30 years ago, American agribusiness company, Archer Daniel Midlands, faced charges of price-fixing in fine chemicals. This led to imprisonment for some officers. The whistle-blower was a senior company officer, Mark Whitacre, who faced constructive dissonance from his wife. He acquiesced with her dissonance and blew the whistle. Likewise, Sophie Zhang and subsequently Frances Haugen, blew the whistle on Facebook's political manipulations because nobody within the company took their constructive dissonance seriously. It was the same case with Dinesh Thakur at Ranbaxy. Neeti and constructive dissonance are valuable for companies and even for governance.

The 'Long Game' As Business Strategy

Indian business leaders tend to be opportunistic rather than strategic, perhaps a hangover from the licence raj. Gurus exhort business leaders to view businesses through a long-term lens. Is business really a long game? What *is* a long game?

In his book *Finite and Infinite Games*[153], Professor James Carse stated that everything in life is a game. Games that have a winner and loser come to an end and conclude, unlike games that you play just for the sake of it. He states that we should become infinite game players. Carse also wrote, 'One does not win by *being powerful*; one wins *to become* powerful. If one has

---

[153]Carse, James, *Finite and Infinite Games*, Free Press, 2011.

enough power to win before the game has begun, what follows is not a game at all.'[154] As an illustration of winning to become powerful, think of NASA as the US's response to USSR's launch of Sputnik first.

Carse differentiates a finite player as being trained to anticipate every move of the competitor, moving the game towards a conclusion by preventing the competitor from altering the past. For example, football is a finite game. Infinite players play in the expectation of being surprised and, therefore, expect the game to continue for long with no winner or loser. A good marriage, for example, is an infinite game.

Simon Sinek, author of the book *The Infinite Game,* offered a corporate example.[155] On one of his visits to Microsoft, he observed that executives were obsessed with competition—to analyse, criticize and decimate competition. Microsoft gifted him a Zune HD, which, according to him, was an exceptional product. Soon after, he visited Apple and mentioned to some managers what an exceptional product Zune HD was. Apple executives thoughtfully responded, 'Really? I reckon we have work to do.' He suggested that Microsoft was in a mindset of playing a finite game, while Apple was playing an infinite game.

Similarly, HUL launched a cream in 1975 to make Indians fair and lovely. The branding and product delivery were both exceptional. Deploying Sinek's ideology, the company entered the five-step virtuous circle—work for a cause, build trusting teams, study worthy rivals, retain existential flexibility and display courage. The company built a ₹4,000 crore skincare brand by extending the product over the next 45 years not only within India but also South Asia, Arab regions, Malaysia and other markets. However, the company's cause had to change because the world changed.

[154]Ibid.

[155]Sinek, Simon, *The Infinite Game*, Penguin Random House, 2019.

Over time, the brand proposition became socially controversial because eulogizing fairness as a beauty attribute became passé. Consequently, the company had to exercise existential flexibility and courage to change. Time will tell whether it succeeded, but one thing is for sure: HUL is playing an infinite game.

Wise business leaders should reflect on how to play the infinite game.

11

··

Reflections: Scepticism, Obliquity and the Trinity

J oseph Jastrow, a Polish–American psychologist, studied the
rabbit–duck illusion. This ambiguous image is perceived
as a duck by some and as a rabbit by others. In Jastrow's
study, many who saw the rabbit could not see the duck even after
being prompted to try and vice versa. In the public domain, one
sees a similar effect playing out between two extremes, like the
Left–liberal intellectuals versus the Right–conservative votaries
in the US, UK, Brazil, Hungary, Italy and more.

Malfeasance or Misjudgement?

The issue of perception raised by the rabbit–duck illusion can be
seen in some cases of corporate misgovernance. A dangerously
high risk-taking CEO could be seen by some directors in a positive
light while other directors may view her as reckless and crazy. Who
can quantify the appropriate level of risk before it crosses over
into the domain of malfeasance? Even among the acknowledged
cases, some perceive malfeasance when it is accompanied by a

mens rea or bad intent, while others view the same as entrepreneurial misjudgement. Of course, when commentaries are written in hindsight, both are clubbed together as heinous crimes committed by greedy businessmen.

Everywhere, enterprise is facing governance headwinds and, sometimes, even existential threats. These threats arise from executive flaws, like excessive borrowing, leadership narcissism, bad strategy, poor management, bad timing, incoherent customer values and unwarranted optimism. It is difficult to separate bad intent from misjudgement.

Overseas, companies like Theranos (and its founder Elizabeth Holmes), Credit Suisse (embroiled in scandals involving spies, lies and money laundering), Volkswagen (Dieselgate) and Wirecard (corrupt business practices and fraudulent financial reporting), have had cases of malfeasance. Many of these companies had stellar directors. Theranos tops the list with global luminaries like Henry Kissinger, George Shultz and General James Mattis. *The Washington Post* bemoaned that these Theranos directors did not pay in any way for overlooking Holmes' fraud.

India, too, has had, and continues to identify, its share of suspicious entrepreneurs. At companies like Satyam, where the CEO lied blatantly or hid facts, the independent directors argued that it had been difficult for them to detect any wrongdoing.

Healthy Scepticism

Independent directors add value to a company, not only through their explicit knowledge and cognitive skills but also through their experiential intuition and heuristic skills. This is easier said than done. Independent directors must develop healthy scepticism, which is born out of curiosity and is quite different from suspicion, which is born out of predisposition or biases. A healthy dose of scepticism adds value to boards. It takes dogged effort to unearth facts, sifting through misstatements, financial misappropriation and misrepresentation of facts, as evidenced by the CG Power case.

Ask journalist John Carreyrou of *The Washington Post* on the Theranos case or prominent Indian journalist Sucheta Dalal who unearthed several security markets scams like Harshad Mehta, Ketan Parekh, NSE co-location and DHFL. Such investigations require healthy scepticism, which turns into suspicion at some stage.

Misgovernance cases teach directors that doing nothing about smoke signals is not an option. Healthy scepticism is a virtue. It is a fundamental tenet of science. As Niels Bohr said, 'The opposite of a fact is falsehood, but the opposite of one profound truth may very well be another profound truth.'[156] Everything is interconnected while being separate. This is the premise of karma—every action has an effect and both are recorded in one's karma. According to the theory of 'quantum entanglement', two particles are linked regardless of the space between them. This can be linked to the butterfly effect, in chaos theory, wherein a small change in one state can result in a large effect on another state.

Similarly, a company is an entanglement of various mutations and transactions. Malfeasance is one end of the spectrum of corporate character, the other end being authentic leadership which is about transparency and fairness. In an inspiring interview, the outgoing CEO of Mars, Grant Reid, described how the company has become less opaque with changing times, all in a planned and conscious manner.[157]

If you are a director of a reckless company, your being there is questionable. If you are a director of an authentic company,

---

[156]'Niels Bohr Quotes', *BrainyQuote*, https://tinyurl.com/59ykcw8r. Accessed on 30 June 2023.

[157]Taylor, Kate, and Clayton Dyer, 'Mars CEO Breaks Down the $35 Billion Transformation of the Company', *Business Insider Video*, 2019, https://tinyurl.com/5emfna9j. Accessed on 5 July 2023.

you are fortunate. In the wide spectrum of in-between companies, directors need to exercise healthy scepticism using scientific tools and actions—observe, hypothesize, experiment and repeat the cycle till a truth emerges.

The Power of Obliquity

Another interesting concept is the principle of obliquity. It is the act of aiming for goals indirectly rather than directly. Several years ago, Gopal came across John Kay's book[158] on the topic, which implies that the world is too complex for our best plans. He remembered obliquity while reading former HUL chief Ashok Ganguly's *Afterness*[159]. Ganguly stated that he never dreamt of becoming a scientist, he never targeted to rise up in his corporate career and he did not aim to serve as a scientific advisor to the prime minister. Yet, all these things happened in his life. He hinted that if we focus diligently on doing what we need to do in our jobs, our career will always progress.

It could happen due to the employer or just sheer luck. Either way, the wisdom of obliquity tends to dawn on us when we have run the course of our careers, and we are looking back at it. Psephologists and economists realize how wrong their prediction models were, business leaders realize how misguided they were about the centrality of their own role in achievements and politicians realize how much empty talk they deployed to seduce their voters. Kay wrote that obliquity 'describes the process of achieving complex objectives indirectly...happiness is where you find it, not where you go in search of it'.[160]

---

[158]Kay, John, *Obliquity: Why Our Goals are Best Achieved Indirectly*, Profile, 2011.
[159]Ganguly, Ashok, *Afterness: Home and Away*, Penguin Random House India, 2022.
[160]Kay, John, *Obliquity: Why Our Goals are Best Achieved Indirectly*, Profile, 2011.

Gopal used to serve on the board of ICI Ltd—it is now a dead company. It used to be regarded as an ideal employer for several decades, based on its goal to serve customers through innovative and responsible application of chemistry and related science, which would lead to the company enhancing the wealth and well-being of various stakeholders. It is a grand example of obliquity. After the 1991 raid by Hanson Trust, ICI revised its commitment by stating that it would enhance value for customers and shareholders through various means.[161]

Although ICI no longer exists, it created great value when it sought shareholders obliquely. Of course, the causes for its success could be many, and obliquity could just be one of them.

Lynn Stout, in her book[162], stated that focussing on the shareholders' interest could be harmful for the corporation. She argued, 'No law has ever required directors of public companies to maximize share price or shareholder wealth.' Quoting Jack Welch, she asserted that shareholder value is not the smartest idea in the world. Is this true? If it is, why would so many corporate leaders aggressively pursue shareholder wealth creation?

Too many managers believe that if you do not seek something directly, you never get it. However, this may not necessarily be true. Jim Collins, an American researcher, author and high priest of business management, found in a study during the 1980s that Sony, which had stated that it would eliminate undue profit-seeking, outperformed HP and Texas Instruments.[163] Likewise, P&G outperformed Colgate and Marriot outperformed Howard Johnson.

[161]Reader, William Joseph, *Imperial Chemical Industries History*, Oxford University Press, 1970.

[162]Stout, Lynn, *The Shareholder Value Myth: How Putting Shareholders First Harms Investors, Corporations, and the Public*, Berrett-Koehler Publishers, 2012.

[163]Collins, Jim, 'Building Companies to Last', *Jim Collins*, 1995, https://tinyurl.com/yzyy4bf6. Accessed on 5 July 2023.

Basically, the company that put *more* emphasis on profit was *less profitable* in its financial performance.

Similarly, Jamsetji Tata never spoke of the Tata Group's profit goals. He emphasized that his enterprises existed because of the community. The total shareholder returns (TSR) of Tata as a group over a decade or more has been ranking around the top of India's corporate sector. Yet, how many financial papers write about long-term TSR?

Some may regard these ideas as relevant for the past but not for the twenty-first century. However, even Kotak Mahindra Bank, one of the banks with the highest price-earning multiples in the world, seeks to provide an ethos of trust. It also seeks to function as a single window to every financial service in a customer's universe and emphasizes that value creation rather than size is its business driver.[164] Now contrast Kotak's obliquity with the more direct goals of the erstwhile YES Bank.

According to philosophical speaker Jaya Row, the Bhagavad Gita offers this road map for success: one should recognize that action is under your control, but the outcome is dependent on factors beyond your control. Fix an ideal beyond your selfish, self-centred interests.[165] For instance, a brilliant and eager student, who is desperate for success in the exams, may suddenly go blank. An outstanding sportsman may fail because of his obsession with the trophy. A job aspirant anxious for a job may fumble in an interview.

Corporate chiefs, especially founders of start-ups, might reconsider the dubious value of corporate statements of purpose, such as, 'Double the market capitalization from X to Y by year

---

[164]'Our Vision', *Kotak Mahindra Bank*, https://tinyurl.com/4fwnv957. Accessed on 5 July 2023.

[165]Row, Jaya, 'Bhagwad Gita Offers a Roadmap for Success', *Speaking Tree*, 3 December 2022, https://tinyurl.com/34jub3s2. Accessed on 5 July 2023.

ABC.' Likewise, national leaders should try setting oblique goals, like delivering rapidly increasing social, judicial and economic justice to the population, in turn improving growth.

Thus, the many virtues of obliquity are worth reflecting upon.

The Trinity Delivers

Media and commentators are smitten by start-ups. Notwithstanding the fact that the criteria for the success of start-ups are hazy, there is a tearing hurry to identify genius, like Sam Bankman-Fried (SBF)—the disgraced founder of the collapsed cryptocurrency exchange FTX. Having commenced operations in 2019, SBF positioned himself as a public intellectual and marketed himself to venture capitalists as a genius eccentric, and they all fell for his charade. He was later accused of stealing customers' deposits to fund operations and investments. SBF's venture should have performed profitably for a reasonable period. It should have been judged by public markets, weathered storms and developed the discipline and genes to evolve into a sustainable, honest enterprise over decades, like Infosys, Biocon, Bharti and Marico, before being declared a success. Therefore, it makes sense to discern success only after several years. S. Ramadorai's book describing the disciplined journey of TCS from a start-up to its IPO stage is a testament to this fact.[166]

With an abundance of cheap money, certain propensities have emerged globally: short-circuiting the natural laws of enterprise evolution, premature celebration of start-ups and hastily tapping public markets. It is pathetic to see so many IPOs floundering at half their issue price.

Mercurial founders get disproportionate public exposure. Overseas, we can take the examples the founders of Tesla, Theranos

---

[166]A. Ramadorai, *The TCS Story & Beyond*, Penguin Books, 2013.

and Meta. In India, there are the founders of Byju's, PayTM and Bharatpe. These founders and whimsical companies have fired employees gracelessly and sponsored high-profile events even while registering massive losses.

On the flip side, there are the long-surviving institutions that have been playing the infinite game: working day in and day out, paying taxes, earning profits, declaring dividends, building a market reputation and painstakingly building companies valued at billions of dollars. They are thought to be less interesting, which, luckily, works to their benefit because nothing pulls down leaders like negative media exposure.

The mercurial and the methodical approaches have remote parallels in the Indian holy trinity. Brahma and Saraswati represent knowledge and innovation. Shiva and Parvati represent power. Vishnu and Lakshmi represent wealth. In any enterprise, innovation, power and wealth are all essential. In Indian mythology, Shiva and Vishnu have more stories told about them than Brahma; they also have more temples. But when it comes to enterprise, media and commentaries devote disproportionate attention to the knowledge and innovation of Brahma (start-ups). While mercurial start-ups do disrupt the system, methodical, long-surviving companies deliver results. Neither needs to be played down. Management leaders blend mercurial Brahma and angry Shiva with methodical Vishnu to build great institutions.

The roles of independent directors, media and regulators are increasingly being rethought. It is difficult for an observer to sense the likelihood of a potential failure, yet some observers do need to do so. Who maintains balance and order in this ecosystem of creation, power and wealth?

There seems to be a pattern in the evolution of most scandals—healthy scepticism reveals unbelievable or suspicious developments; then, the board, regulator or media investigates and perhaps conviction follows; finally, a book and a film is made about the incident.

In the case of the 'magical' German fintech company, Wirecard, a shareholder association raised initial doubts. *Financial Times* cottoned on to the emerging fraud and a film called *Skandal! Bringing Down Wirecard* was made about the incident.

In India, investigative business journalism could be sharper, along with swifter regulatory and conviction processes. There is also an expectation of a greater effectiveness from independent directors who need to build an attitude of healthy scepticism, which can be a life-enhancing virtue for all.

Directors should hold top leadership up to the following behaviours.

1. **Credibility**: Is the person believable?
2. **Reliability**: Does the person deliver?
3. **Intimacy**: Does one feel comfortable with the person?
4. **Perception**: Is the leader too self-focussed?

Some CEOs do not live up to these behavioural standards. Imagine how the YES Bank CEO would fare on this test before its collapse.

While most CEOs and founders regard themselves as geniuses, only a miniscule fit the bill. Most of them tend to have an exaggerated opinion of themselves. Thus, independent directors, apart from media and regulators, can play a steadying role in corporations.

12

Epilogue: The Fly-on-the-Wall Observer

There are many books and papers on corporate governance. They usually dwell on disasters and misdemeanours of a gross nature. After the unravelling of the case, the perpetrators are depicted as evil-eyed plotters, which may be true in some cases but, in many, the facts are distorted to match a linear reality. It is not easy to separate bad intent from entanglement, as the examples below suggest.

In the Tata Finance scandal of 1999–2000, was Dilip Pendse a congenial crook? Many who knew Pendse, would vigorously doubt that. They might argue that he perhaps did take one trade too far to match his vaulting ambitions, which turned out to be the deal that went wrong. Then, to make up for that loss, more unwise deals were perhaps made until the whole situation spiralled out of his control.

It is the same belief shared by many about the Ramalinga Raju and the Satyam case in 2008. Infotech professionals who knew Raju insist that he was not a scheming person. His was a genuine rags-to-riches story. At some stage, most likely, his ambition exceeded his grasp on reality, leading him to real-estate deals that eventually sank him. Similarly, in 2019, Café Coffee Day's story of debt and business pressures unravelled after the tragic suicide of founder V.G. Siddhartha.

More recently, CG Power and Industrial Systems known as Crompton Greaves, under the stewardship of Gautam Thapar, was a professionally run and highly competent company. Thapar assimilated Crompton into a clutch of companies, grouped together under the name of Avantha Group.

CG Power had an exemplary board, which was ever watchful and invested its time in a potentially prized company of the future. In 2019, the independent directors noted that the apparently improving earnings before interest, taxes, depreciation and amortization (EBITDA) did not result in commensurate cash flows and profit before tax (PBT). They treated this as a smoke signal.

The risk and audit committee, steered by independent directors, delved into the details with some healthy scepticism. They were astounded to stumble on to surprise after surprise that had slipped their diligence and professionalism. They discovered a complex web of related parties, which meant interconnected subsidiaries. There were many loan transactions among those companies. Thapar had apparently availed loans from a consortium of 13 banks against the same securities without disclosing finances and understating the company's liabilities. In every listed company board, the independent directors will never know the detail of the domain or transactions that company managements have at their fingertips. This asymmetry of knowledge is a fact of life.

The risk and audit committee, unaware of the facts, was confronted with a web of transactions among related companies. These were glibly explained by the operating management through some slick arguments that assailed the common sense of the independent directors, who delved further. After a 13-hour meeting, they put the pieces together and were startled with the facts that emerged. The total liabilities of the company and the group were understated by ₹1,990 crores and ₹2,800 crores, respectively. Advances to related companies amounted to ₹2,657 crore and not just ₹131 crore, as had been officially reported in the accounts. Certain employees had made multiple unauthorized transactions, which had hugely impacted the company's finances.[167]

Meanwhile, what was visible in the public domain was that the stock price of the company had shrunk by 70 per cent of its value in the past few months. The board blew the whistle on itself when it convened thereafter. The promoter–chairman was sacked, the regulatory authorities were invited in, and the painful cleaning-up process, as per equity and law had started. There are several cases that bear a close resemblance to the CG Power case.

In many of the cases discussed above, and in other such episodes, people around the mastermind observed a behavioural change in them but did not treat it as a smoke signal.

The Fly on the Wall

To continually improve boards, the tick box method provides some data. However, it tells only part of the story. There is no one available as a neutral, fly-on-the-wall observer who can unravel the intricacies of interpersonal relationships and collaboration versus competitiveness instincts. Who can hold a mirror, true and faithful, up to the behavioural dynamics of the board as a whole?

The chairman of a reputed company approached Gopal to work with his board and senior leadership team to unravel the true potential of the talent on the board and senior team. Gopal worked with about 30 senior and experienced individuals as a

[167]Jain, Anisha, 'CG Power: Curious Case of Misstatements and Financial Fraud', *CNBC TV18*, 20 August 2019, https://tinyurl.com/yc5ja5ec. Accessed on 5 July 2023.

board advisor for several months. The client company was happy to not only pay the fees but also to soldier on with addressing the perceptual and psychological blockages diluting their potential impact. At the end of the engagement, it was a win–win, as everyone was satisfied that the process had been effective.

One would assume that a great board would include the best professionals. Indeed, regulations are also based on this belief: surely, distinguished professionals from bureaucracy and management must make effective board members. However, this is only the case if their mind is prepared for the job. The best people need to be melded to be effective—they need to be a team, like in sports. A group of personally accomplished, non-team-players are likely to cause dysfunction. Sports teams have coaches and mentors, so do modern top executives, but boards do not.

Boards can be noisy parliaments and might even appear dysfunctional due to conflicting views. Depending on personality, some board members do not speak up at all, some do so politely while others argue forcefully. Boards do not necessarily have a harmonious atmosphere, never mind the mythology that promotes such an image. As we reflect on boards, the influence of human behaviour on board processes flash through our minds. In this context, two anecdotes are relevant.

On one board, the company chairman piloted a proposal to invest in an unrelated diversification. Owing to this, even the more influential directors hesitated to oppose the proposal. A feisty and argumentative director, however, known to be a chairman–confidante, opposed the proposal vehemently to the great relief of the other directors.

In another company, an ambitious CEO created the perception among his board that his edgy proposals had prior assent of a powerful promoter non-director. One day, they discovered that the edgy schemes were a massive fraud. It was a pity that the edgy schemes had gone unchallenged until then.

As every director has experienced, human foibles—ego, rivalry, crucial silence, treating directorship as a privilege and so on—dominate board functioning.

Directors can benefit themselves and their companies from either training themselves, or being formally trained to embrace behavioural principles and group dynamics. There is always a place for board coaching by a wise and experienced person, acting as a fly on the wall. Such a person can help ease the inevitable dysfunctions in board dynamics. While boards engage with rational, left-brain matters, there is still a place for affection, esteem and warmth.

Here are some critical soft skills that all directors must acquire.

1. How to balance operational and strategic issues.
2. How to disagree without becoming disagreeable.
3. How to speak up when it really matters.
4. How to genuinely listen to alternate views without being judgemental.
5. When to be transactional and when to be reflective.
6. How to avoid relapsing into delusional memories of your days as the big chief.

The dawn of a new era for good corporate governance is underway. Corporate India needs wise and experienced directors who are not just active on boards, but who can also sit in board meetings as a fly on the wall. They can do for collective boards what executive coaches do for ascendant executives. Just a decade ago, having a personal coach was considered derogatory to the executive. Within a decade, trained coaches of varying competence have emerged. These days, executives wear their coaches as a badge of pride. Such a skill has developed in boards across Europe and the US and may become relevant in a few years as an aid to India Inc.

This book has been written to plant the idea that board effectiveness, like quality control, is a line leader's job. Senior leaders must take an all-of-system approach over a unidimensional one. As a consequence of this thought, we hope that the idea of a reliable fly-on-the-wall consultant will also emerge soon.

In conclusion, we hope that we have succeeded in prising open the black box of behaviour in the boardroom, and offering a few perspectives for readers.

Acknowledgements

We would like to thank Rupa Publications for their constant encouragement and deep involvement in the writing of this book. Kapish Mehra and Yamini Chaudhuri have for long expressed deep interest in this subject, especially suggesting that we adopt a narrative style rather than a regulatory style. The Rupa team has been a source of strength in editing the copy, and contributed to designing an excellent cover.

We are deeply grateful for the perceptive review of the initial manuscript, especially from Dr Ashok S. Ganguly, former chairman of HLL. We are also grateful for the comments and endorsements provided for the book by Sanjiv Mehta, N. Chandrasekaran, M. Damodaran and Omkar Goswami.

Co-authoring a book poses its own challenges. We would like to thank each other for mutual collaboration and collegial patience in crafting this important book.

Gopal would like to acknowledge the influence of his many board colleagues—over 100 of them—with whom he has been on 20-odd boards over 35 years. In their own subtle ways, each of them has influenced the thinking underlying this book. On a personal note, Gopal would like to thank his wife, Geeta, for her patience and quiet encouragement.

Tulsi would like to thank her husband, Jay, and her daughter, Radhika, who have supported her and been her greatest cheerleaders through her academic endeavours and professional pursuits.

Index